D0854225

THE
SOVIET PLANNED
ECONOMIC ORDER

By WILLIAM HENRY CHAMBERLIN

AMS PRESS
NEW YORK

Reprinted from the edition of 1931, Boston
First AMS EDITION published 1969
Manufactured in the United States of America

Library of Congress Catalog Card Number: 70-107342
SBN: 404-00595-0

AMS PRESS, INC.
New York, N.Y. 10003

INTRODUCTION

THE Soviet Union to-day is a most inviting and comprehensive field of research for the economics student. A country whose territory occupies over one seventh of the surface of the globe is reorganizing its whole economic life along socialist lines, discarding and repudiating many of the accepted laws of capitalist economy. Quite possibly the future historian will regard the Soviet experiment in planned economics as one of the most important events of the twentieth century.

A detailed history of Soviet economic development might easily reach encyclopedic proportions. In the present work I have tried to show how the element of planning assumed steadily larger proportions in Soviet life, culminating in the adoption of the Five-Year Plan of national development, and how this plan has functioned in operation. My sources of information have been threefold:

Soviet books, magazines and newspapers; personal observation and study of living and working conditions in town and country, and conversations with Soviet officials and experts in the economic departments of the state.

In this connection I am glad to acknowledge my gratitude and indebtedness to representatives of the All-Union and All-Russian State Planning Commissions and of the Supreme Economic Council, both for information which they communicated to me orally and for their kind assistance in procuring economic books of reference. Of course, I alone am responsible for the selections which I made from the material at my disposal and, in general, for the interpretative aspects of the work.

WILLIAM HENRY CHAMBERLIN.

Moscow, January 16, 1931.

CONTENTS

APPENDICES

CONTENTS

THE SOVIET PLANNED
ECONOMIC ORDER

CHAPTER I

SOVIET STATE ECONOMIC PLANNING: ORIGIN AND BACKGROUNDS

ONE of the main theoretical arguments in favor of socialism has always been the possibility of planning and ordering the whole economic life of a nation under this system and hence avoiding the recurrent crises of the competitive capitalist system. It is natural, therefore, that the Soviet Government, which professes to be guided by Marxian socialism in all its activities, should have made a serious effort to realize in fact the theories of national economic planning which had hitherto been a matter of more or less Utopian speculation. However, it is only within the last two or three years, and especially since

1

the inauguration of the Five-Year Plan of national development in 1928, that the element of planning began to dominate all branches of Soviet economic life.

When the Bolsheviki seized power in Russia and set up the Soviet form of government in November, 1917, they did not, so far as one can judge from the relevant decrees, intend or desire to socialize all branches of national economic life immediately. Banks and transportation were nationalized rather quickly and foreign trade was declared a state monopoly. In regard to industry, however, the Soviet Government at first abstained, as a general rule, from the direct transference of plants from private to state ownership and operation, limiting itself to the issue of a decree which gave the factory committees, elected by the workers, certain rights of consultation and control in respect to management.

The first Soviet Land Law vested title to land in the state and proclaimed the confiscation of the estates of the larger landowners, the Tsarist family and the Church. The right to use land, within such limits as local conditions might impose, was granted to all citizens of the so-called toiling classes. In practice this law simply completed and legalized a process that had been going on with varying degrees of thoroughness and intensity ever since the downfall of Tsarism in March, 1917: the confiscation of the larger estates and the division of the land among the peasants, who were guided to a greater or less degree by the traditional rule of the Russian village that larger families were intitled to larger shares of the village land. There was no serious attempt at the beginning of the Revolution to force state and cooperative forms of farming upon the peasants.

The system of workers' control in industry broke down because few owners were willing or able to carry on operations under such an arrangement. So, as some factories were abandoned by their owners, while in other cases the workers themselves drove away the managers and engineers, the state was obliged to take them over. This process of piecemeal nationalization was greatly accelerated in the summer of 1918, when the state took over almost all the large and medium sized industrial plants. In no small degree this was an emergency war measure. The existence of the Soviet state was menaced by foreign intervention and internal rebellion. The factory owners as a class were naturally unsympathetic with the new régime, and the taking over of the factories, for which the Soviet Government was really economically unprepared, was advocated as a necessary measure for limiting the possibilities of treason and sabotage.

Further steps in the direction of state regimentation of economic life were taken in 1920, after the first phase of the civil war had ended victoriously for the Soviet Government with the defeat of Kolchak, Denikin and Yudenich. The principle of universal liability for labor service received legal sanction and application, and some of the armies which were no longer needed on the fronts were held together as labor armies and performed under military or semi-military discipline such tasks as cutting wood, digging peat, etc. The outbreak of the war with Poland in the spring of 1920 put an end to these experiments in militarized labor, which were not particularly successful from the standpoint of productivity.

During the civil war any organized or detailed planning of Russian economic life was made impossible by the shifting fortunes of the battlefield. Important industrial regions and sources of raw material changed hands. Provision for the needs of the army was the first and fundamental objective of the Soviet industries. There could be no question of undertaking new large scale public works.

4

The first germ of the later system of state economic planning may, however, be seen, in the institution in February, 1920, of the State Commission for the Electrification of Russia. This commission worked during the year and laid before the Eighth Congress of Soviets, which met in December, 1920, a plan for the establishment throughout Russia of a network of electrical stations, designed to stimulate the growth of industry and agriculture. The commission reached the conclusion that Soviet Russia must be divided into districts along economic lines, " predecessors of the future flourishing communes of the developed order of freed labor." The commission furthermore based its conclusions upon the following propositions:

The sole road of escape from economic ruin is the increase in the shortest possible time of the productivity of the people's labor with the minimum expenditure of labor units and material resources. . . . Analysis shows that the most promising instrument for the intensification, mechanization and rationalization of labor is the electrification of the economic life of the country. Therefore electrification must be the basic idea of our economic construction.

The plan was accepted by the Soviet Congress and received the enthusiastic indorsement of Lenin, who always cherished the idea that the widespread introduction of electrical energy under socialized control might serve the double purpose of facilitating the introduction of socialist forms of organization and overcoming Russia's technical backwardness, which had been, of course, enhanced by the havoc and isolation from the outside world caused by the Revolution and civil war.

However, although the Goelro, or State Commission for the Electrification of Russia, represented the beginning of the idea of state planning that later found expression in the Gosplan, or State Planning Commission, and although its scheme of electrification bore some remote resemblance to the subsequent more precisely calculated and detailed Five-Year Plans, circumstances were not favorable at that time for the practical realization of large scale projects of planned economic development.

It would be difficult to exaggerate the economic prostration of Russia [1] after six and a half years of continuous international and civil war, combined with social revolution and blockade. In-

[1] Russia is no longer a term properly applicable to the country. Since January, 1924, the central government has been that of the Union of Soviet Socialist Republics, of which the Russian Soviet Socialist Republic is the principal unit. As it is also that part of the territory of the Union in which the Five-Year Plan is most assiduously being developed, it will occur frequently in the following pages that conditions in that republic will be referred to in particular. Where conditions applicable to the whole Soviet Union are referred to, care has been taken to use that term.

dustrial output had sunk to 15 or 20% of the 1913 figure and the production of some of the basic metals was as low as 2%. Agricultural production had shrunk to 55% of the pre-war average and the drought of 1921, together with the contraction of the planted area and the exhaustion of food reserves, was destined to bring a terrific famine on the land. There had been a tremendous exodus from the cities because of the lack of food and the industrial working class was scattered all over the country.

During the years of civil war it had proved quite impossible to reach any firm basis of economic collaboration with the peasants. The shrinking supplies of industrial goods were largely earmarked for the army. In order to supply the hungry cities with an indispensable minimum of bread the authorities were obliged to resort to requisitions, which irritated the peasants and led to local disturbances and to an increasing diminution of the planted area. Experiments were made during this period with forms of agriculture of which much more will be heard later, of state farms and communes or cooperative farms, formed by groups of peasants. But not only was there a vast weight of instinctive peasant antipathy to nonindividualist farming methods to overcome, but the mechanical basis for successful large scale farms — tractors and large machines — was quite lacking.

The Kronstadt uprising in March, 1921, and continual unrest in the peasant districts convinced the Soviet leaders that some drastic immediate change of policy must be adopted in order to start the curve of production, which had declined to an almost impossibly low point, upward again. The New Economic Policy, first outlined by Lenin in a speech before the Tenth Congress of the Communist Party in March, 1921, and amplified by various subsequent decrees, represented such a change.

An individualist stimulus to production was restored to the peasants by the substitution of a fixed tax in kind (later replaced by a money tax) for the requisitions and by reestablishing freedom of internal trade. Simultaneously the iron hold which the Soviet state had established over the lives of its citizens during the period of so-called "war communism" was appreciably relaxed in various directions. Labor conscription was dropped and one heard no more of the labor armies. A currency system was gradually built up and internal stabilization of the ruble was achieved early in 1924. Private shops, abolished during the epoch of war communism, reopened, and markets, which had dragged out a harassed semi-legal existence, began to flourish. Private traders and speculators, the so-called Nepmen, began to appear.

The state retained possession and operation of the basic industries, but methods of administration were considerably changed with a view to giving greater authority and responsibility to each state trust for the management of the factories under its control. The impossibly bureaucratic, highly centralized system of managing the state industries was modified in the direction of giving the individual trusts, which were placed in charge of groups of factories, greater autonomy and greater responsibility in their industrial and commercial operations.

Under the triple influence of the Nep, as the New Economic Policy came to be known, the favorable harvests of 1922 and 1923 and the cessation of war and internal disturbance, the Soviet Union began to recover visibly. The cities began to fill again; idle factories were gradually placed in operation; the general standard of living rose.

This recovery, in its first stages, had little to do with state planning. It was rather an elemental process, not responsive to deliberate guidance. A central state board could not plan accurately the activities of the individual peasant producer or of the elusive Nepman; and even the state trusts and the cooperative stores, in the first years of the Nep, were regulated by the immediate demands of the market more than by theoretical projects, designed to cover a term of years.

At first the Nep was often interpreted outside of the Soviet Union as the beginning of a return to full-fledged capitalism. But the fallaciousness of this view became clearer with the passing of years. The limitations of the Nep, in the long run, proved more significant than its concessions to private enterprise and private profit. In the first place the Soviet state retained its hold on the basic things in Russian economic life: industry, transport, banking and the monopoly of foreign trade. The influence of the Nepmen was largely restricted to the field of retail trade, a field from which they could be and were gradually pushed out as the cooperative system gained in strength and scope and as the Soviet authorities applied a more and more ruthless system of economic and administrative pressure against the private merchant.

In the second place foreign capital did not flow into the Soviet Union to any considerable extent after the adoption of the Nep. The failure to reach any agreement regarding foreign claims in respect to prewar debts and nationalized property and the limitations which Soviet legislation imposed upon foreign industrial and commercial activity in the Soviet Union discouraged, as a rule, direct investment of foreign capital. This failure to attract foreign capital made the process of Soviet economic reconstruction somewhat slower and more difficult than it might otherwise have been; but it also left the Soviet Government free to pursue socialist economic policies without the complications and conflicts which would most probably have ensued if large foreign interests, enjoying the political support of their governments, had been directly affected by such policies.

Another potential source of capitalist revival in the Union was the individual peasant owner. Here, too, however, the Soviet system imposed definite limitations upon the development of the more prosperous peasants, the so-called *kulaks*. The latter, under the conditions of the first years of the Nep, might raise themselves somewhat above the level of their fellows by the exercise of greater shrewdness, thrift and farming capacity. But the legal prohibition of the purchase and sale of land and the Communist agrarian policy of repressing the richer peasants through taxation and other discriminations prevented the *kulaks* from developing into a new class of small landlords, with farms running into the hundreds of acres.

Political and general factors also facilitated the transition from the looser reconstruction methods of the early years of the Nep to a more definite system of state planning, which, in turn, involved a suppression of the capitalist elements in Soviet economic life in favor of the socialist. Planning with any approach to accuracy presupposes control of the field for which the plan is made, and it is no accidental coincidence that the growth of state planning has been in very close relation to the elimination of private enterprise and initiative, first in trade and then in agriculture.

Among these political and general factors were the steady permeation of the population, especially of the industrial workers, with Communist ideas through the Soviet Government's monopolistic control of schools and newspapers and the various agencies of agitation and propaganda which the Communist Party created, and the completion of the reconstruction process in Soviet economic life — i. e., the reattainment of the 1913 level of output in agriculture and industry. Another important element in the situation was the campaign of a faction in the Communist Party, headed by Leon Trotzky, against the policies of the party leadership.

The Trotzkyists emphasized very strongly the alleged growth of the Nepman and the *kulak* and depicted the country as being in danger of a reversion to capitalism. While the Trotzkyists were ultimately expelled from the party and those of them who refused to recant were in many cases arrested and exiled, the final blow which the astute leader of the majority group in the party leadership, Joseph Stalin, delivered against these opponents was the adoption of a policy which, as regards highspeed industrialization and the elimination of the *kulaks* as a class, was more sweeping, ruthless and ambitious than any of Trotzky's oppositionist suggestions.

One of the first signs that the Soviet Government was contemplating a more organized and planned system of national economic life was the publication in 1925 of " control figures " for the year 1925–1926. (Up till very recently, when the economic year was made to coincide with the calendar year, the Soviet economic year was reckoned from October to October.) These control figures indicated the projected achievements of the ensuing year in such fields as industrial output, investment of capital in industry, agriculture, transport and electrification, movement of prices, production costs, labor productivity, etc.

In 1926 a more ambitious effort was made to work out a five-year plan of economic development. This *pyatiletka* (the Russian expression for Five-Year Plan) was soon supplanted by the Five-Year Plan for 1928–1933, which has exerted such a tremendous influence upon the Soviet Union's development during the last two years; but the underlying ideas of state economic planning were already formulated pretty clearly. G. M. Krzhizhanovsky, the Communist engineer who until very recently was president of the State Planning Commission, in his introduction to the Five-Year Plan of 1926–1931, defined the aim of this plan as " such a redistribution of the existing productive forces of society, including therein both the labor power and the material resources of the country, as would guarantee in the highest degree the output of these productive forces without crises at the quickest possible tempo for the purpose of achieving the maximum satisfaction of the current needs of the toilers, and of bringing them as quickly as possible to the complete reorganization of society on the bases of socialism and communism."

Discussing the feasibility of economic planning Mr. Krzhizhanovsky argues that although perfect accuracy may not be obtainable, just as it is mathematically impossible to square the circle, a satisfactory approximation to accuracy is practicable. Of course, the control figures for each year are capable of more close calculation than the computations based on a five-year period or the still longer plans, based on ten- or fifteen-year periods, which are under contemplation.

The choice of five years as the period of planning was based largely on two considerations. Russia in the past has averaged one poor harvest in every five years, so that reckonings based on this term take this factor into account. Then, a period of five years is considered sufficient to permit the completion of large scale, new construction projects. Mr. Krzhizhanovsky writes:

" The basic problem of the Five-Year Plan is to define the possible dimensions of capital investments for the ensuing five-year period in general and to give a concrete basis for operating programs of financing long term construction projects, designed for the five-year period, in particular."

It would be a grave error to interpret the present or any future Soviet five-year plan as a sort of blue print for the millennium or to believe that its fulfillment would necessarily lead to an immediate, striking and visible change in the country's welfare and standard of living. Changes of various kinds will undoubtedly accompany the progressive realization of the Soviet projects of high-speed industrialization of the country and collectivization of agriculture. Such changes are already visible. But there is no mystical significance about the conclusion of any given five-year period. It will merely be succeeded by a new planned five-year period.

Communist economists do not claim any very high degree of validity for the charts and tables showing how many oil wells will be drilled, how many agricultural machines will be manufactured and how many rubles will be deposited in savings banks five years hence. There are some factors which the most flawless technique of planning can not anticipate: weather conditions, affecting various crops; the movement of world prices, affecting the sums received in payment for exports; new inventions, which may modify the functioning of industries; discoveries of new sources of mineral wealth, which may divert projected schemes of development into new channels. What the Five-Year Plan does, as its advocates would contend, is to mark out a general line of development and to set certain goals of achievement at which to aim. If experience shows, as has been the case in some fields in the Soviet Union, that the projected figures are too low they can be raised, or the term within which the plan should be realized can be shortened.

As planning has come to dominate Soviet economic life more and more thoroughly the Gosplan, or State Planning Commission, has assumed a position of correspondingly enhanced importance among Soviet institutions. It is here that data are collected and the voluminous plans which guide the nation's economic development are formulated, receiving final authority after they have been approved by the Government. The material on which the Gosplan bases its projects is supplied by government departments, state industrial enterprises, state and collective farm units and similar organizations and institutions, which submit their proposed plans of future work. One of the main tasks of the Gosplan is to organize this mass of material and to bring the various projects into harmony with general industrial, agricultural and financial policies.

The Gosplan is one of the committees of the Sto, or Council of Labor and Defense, which is a sort of economic cabinet. The 22 members of the presidium, or governing board of the Gosplan, are appointed by the Government, and the head of this presidium holds the office of Vice-Premier of the Soviet Union. The work of the Gosplan is coordinated by a bureau of national economic planning and the Gosplan includes eleven sections, whose functions may briefly be outlined as follows:

1. The Power Section has charge of fuel and electricity. It draws up an account of the power resources of the country and prepares projects for their exploitation. It also draws up a fuel plan and a plan of electrification.

2. The Industrial Section works out the final control figures for industrial output. It is divided into several subsections, specializing in the metal, chemical, lumber, textile and other individual industries.

3. The Agricultural Section draws up plans for the extension of the planted acreage, the allotment of seeds and fodder to various districts and generally gives guidance to the state and collective farms.

4. The Building Section has charge of general construction plans, works out projects for new cities, establishes construction standards and endeavors to insure an adequate supply of building

18

materials for municipal and industrial construction.

5. The Section of Transport and Communication has for its province the preparation of plans for the railroad and water transport systems and also for the development of postal, telegraphic and telephone communication.

6. The Section of Consumption and Distribution prepares projects for the development and extension of the consumers' cooperative stores, which constitute the main agency of retail trade in the Soviet Union; plans the distribution of goods, and also works out construction schemes where there is a connection with the problem of food supply, such as the building of refrigerator plants.

7. The Section of Labor and Trained Experts calculates the need for, and the supply of, engineers, trained experts, skilled and unskilled laborers, and tries to establish a balance between supply and demand by projecting schools and courses where engineers and technicians may be trained and where workers may acquire more skill at their trades. This section also has charge of such problems as wages, growth of productivity of labor, social insurance, labor protective rules.

8. The Section of Culture plans the develop-

ment of schools and works out measures calculated to eliminate illiteracy. Within the sphere of this section come the plans connected with newspapers, libraries, clubs, reading rooms, radio stations, moving picture theaters and other agencies which the Soviet Government endeavors to utilize for " raising the cultural level " of the adult population.

9. The Section of Science attempts to regulate and project scientific research and activity. It decides which scientific institutions are to be preferred in the matter of state subsidies and gives first consideration in that connection to those institutions which pursue definitely utilitarian objectives. It gives directions and suggestions for the exploration and investigation of the natural resources of the country.

10. The Section of Economics and Statistics concentrates in its hands the centralized collection of statistical material which is so essential to the work of the Gosplan.

11. The Organization Section plans the work of the Gosplan itself and the system of selecting its experts and employees. This section expects to create an academy for the training of Gosplan workers.

The Gosplan also maintains an Institute of

Economic Investigation which studies, along with various economic questions, the methodology of planning. This institute decides how the plan is to be made, into what sections it is to be divided and similar matters. It also conducts research in such fields as credit and currency problems, the effects of " socialist competition " and other expedients, which, as will be described later, have been introduced with a view to stimulating greater efficiency and productivity.

The Gosplan has 1,020 employees, of whom 470 are regarded as experts, the remainder representing the clerical force. Its plans of industrial output begin to assume form in the individual factories, each of which submits a production plan to the state trust which is responsible for its management. The trust works out its plan, based on those of its subordinate factories and passes it on to the " union " of all the trusts in the given industries. The union, in turn, transmits its plan to the Supreme Economic Council, which exercises general supervision over all the state industries. The Supreme Economic Council then presents to the Gosplan its control figures of industrial development for the coming year, which the Gosplan subjects to examination and revision, endeavoring to obtain as high a level of production as is compatible with the fuel, raw material and financial resources at the disposal of the state.

The projects of the Gosplan, once they have received the stamp of governmental approval, may not be challenged, and every factory, state or collective farm is bound to put forth its utmost efforts to fulfill the tasks which have been prescribed. If a factory decides that it can better the Gosplan figures by increase of output, by reduction of production costs, or by some other means without requiring additional financial appropriations, so much the better. On the other hand, suggested improvements which require additional financial outlay must be referred back to the Gosplan and the Government for confirmation.

The *pyatiletka* which the Gosplan prepared for the years 1926–1931 attracted comparatively little attention. It was reckoned on a basis of a comparatively moderate rate of progress in industry and agriculture. But the *pyatiletka* of 1928–1933 has excited reverberations around the world. Both because of the visible changes which it has brought into everyday life and because of the tremendous propaganda through the press, through books, through the theater, through lectures, plays, moving picture productions and every other agency for influencing the mind of the public, it is unlikely that even the least literate citizen of the Soviet Union has escaped some shadowy idea of the tremendous process of planned economic reconstruction through which the country is passing.

The Five-Year Plan of 1928–1933 was made up in two variations, a maximum and a minimum. Inasmuch, however, as even the maximum variation has been considerably exceeded in most branches of industrial production during the first two years of the execution of the plan, one need consider only that deviation in describing the main outlines of the project.

The outstanding feature of the *pyatiletka* was the intensive speed of the drive toward industrialization which it marked out. By the end of 1927–28 the Soviet Union had exceeded the prewar level of industrial output by 19.6% and the 1913 level of agricultural production by 5.6%. It is noteworthy, in this connection, that agriculture, which attained the prewar level of output in 1925–26, made little progress during the next two years, whereas industry, which had fallen much lower than agriculture during the prostration of the civil war period, recovered at a much faster rate. By 1928 there were clear evidences of a disproportion between the agricultural and industrial lines of development, and agriculture was failing to supply enough food and raw material to provide for the needs of the expanding industries and the increasing number of workers employed in them.

Starting from this basis the Five-Year Plan proposed to increase the value of the total volume of industrial production (giving the ruble an artificially standardized value for purposes of comparison) from 18,300,000,000 rubles in 1927–28 to 43,200,000,000 rubles in 1933.[1] Production in the basic industries, listed under the so-called Group A (coal, oil, metallurgy, machine-building, etc.) was to be more than trebled; production in the Group B industries, which produce articles of everyday consumption, was to be more than doubled. Russia's coal output, which was 35,400,000 tons in 1927–28, was to reach 75,000,000 tons in 1932–33. The volume of oil production was to increase from 11,800,000 tons in 1927–28 to 21,700,000 tons in 1932–33. By 1932–33 the Soviet Union was to turn out 10,000,000 tons of pig iron, instead of the 3,300,000 tons produced in 1927–28. The output of electric power was to grow from 5,160,000,000 kilowatt hours in 1927–

[1] Authority for all the following statistical statements is to be found in volume 1 *he Five-Year Plan of National Economic Construction of the Soviet Union*, publ by Planned Economic Life, Moscow.

28 to 22,000,000,000 kilowatt hours in 1932–33. The output of agricultural machines, under the Five-Year Plan, was to increase by four times; that of bricks by five times; that of cement by three and a third times. An especially sweeping plan of development was prepared for the comparatively insignificant Russian chemical industry: thus, the end of the Five-Year Plan was to witness an increase in the production of superphosphates by twenty-three times, and of sulphuric acid by seven times.

In agriculture the value of production in stabilized rubles was to rise from 16,600,000,000 rubles in 1927–28 to 25,800,000,000 rubles in 1932–33. The planted acreage was to grow by 22%, the area under grain crops by 15 or 17%, and the area under other crops by 51 or 61%. An important change in the forms of agriculture was also forecast. In 1927–28 98% of the total planted area was farmed by individual peasants, 1.1% by state farms and 0.9% by collective farms, organized by groups of peasants who pooled their land, working animals and machinery on a cooperative basis. In 1932–33, according to the maximum variation of the Five-Year Plan, 14.3% of the planted area should belong to collective farms and 3.5% to state farms. Because of their higher productivity these two forms of socialized farming were expected to supply 42.9% of the marketable surplus grain of the country.

In transport the length of the railroad lines was supposed to grow from 77,000 kilometers in 1927–28 to 90,000 kilometers in 1932–33, and the amount of freight carried from 151,000,000 tons in 1927–28 to 281,000,000 tons in 1932–33.

This very ambitious program of building was supposed to be financed out of the internal accumulations of the country, and especially by a reduction of 32 or 35% in costs of production. Productivity of labor was supposed to grow faster than wages, so that a margin would be left for accumulation and reinvestment in state enterprises. The maximum variation of the plan called for an increase of labor productivity by 110%, while the minimum variation reckoned with an increase of 95%. Nominal wages were to increase by 38%, and real wages by 53% or 66%, depending on whether the cost of living was reduced by 10%, as the minimum variation required, or by 14%, as the maximum variation demanded.

Capital investments in the main branches of economic life were supposed to be distributed as follows for the five-year period: industry, 16,353,-

000,000 rubles; agriculture, 23,152,000,000; electrification, 3,059,000,000; transport, 10,002,000,000.

The Five-Year Plan envisaged an enormous amount of new industrial construction. A plant with a capacity of 50,000 tractors a year was projected in Stalingrad; and, as the need for tractors to equip the rapidly increasing state and collective farms became more pressing, two similar plants were planned, one in Cheliabinsk and the other in Kharkov. The largest agricultural machinery factory in Europe was to be built in Rostov. A factory with a capacity of 140,000 automobiles and trucks a year was designed for Nizhni Novgorod.

To solve the shortage of iron and steel, which had made itself felt even before the ambitious building projects of the Five-Year Plan were formulated, two large new steel plants were to be erected in Magnitogorsk, in the Urals, and in the Kuznetzk Basin, in Siberia. A railroad was projected to permit the utilization of the vast coal resources of the Kuznetzk Basin as a source of supply for the Magnitogorsk plant. Among the numerous electric power plants which were to supply a quadrupled volume of electrical energy the largest was Dnieprstroi, a huge combination hydroelectric power plant and dam on the lower reaches of the River Dnieper. The longest of the new railroads required under the Five-Year Plan was the so-called Turksib, which united a southern spur of the Trans-Siberian line with an eastern branch of the Moscow-Tashkent Railroad and made it possible to transport the grain and lumber of Siberia by a direct route to the cotton regions of Turkestan, besides opening up for development the vast rolling steppes of Kazakstan, an enormous region of Soviet Central Asia which stretches from the frontier of China to the Caspian Sea.

These constituted only a few of the big new undertakings which it was supposed would contribute to the rapid industrialization of the Soviet Union.

The Five-Year Plan called for rapid production of engineers, technicians and skilled workers as well as of plants and machinery. It was estimated that the number of engineers employed in Soviet industry in 1927–28 must be doubled by the end of the Five-Year Plan, while the number of technicians must be trebled. This led to a reorganization of the courses in the universities and higher technical schools in the direction of greater specialization, and to an expansion of the number of students received into these institutions.

The Five-Year Plan of 1928–33 was adopted by the Soviet Government in its maximum variation and received final official confirmation at the Fifth All-Union Congress of Soviets in May, 1929, after it had already been in effect for about eight months. The presidium of the Gosplan characterized it as " a plan of great works and of developed socialist offensive."

Its significance was perhaps even greater than its framers imagined. The adoption of this huge project, more, perhaps, than any other development, marked the transition from the relatively loose and easygoing system of the Nep, with its various concessions to private initiative, to a much more tense, strictly regimented and definitely socialist phase of the Revolution, where many of the earlier concessions to the instinct for private gain were annulled and others were strongly limited.

For the tendencies which the Five-Year Plan indicated and helped to set in motion — the rapid industrialization of the country, the introduction and extension of socialist methods in agriculture — moved faster than the original schedule had required. Before the first year of the plan had been completed, the slogan " The Five-Year Plan in four years " was proclaimed. The final date of the plan was more or less officially moved up from October 1, 1933, to October 1, 1932. Then in the latter part of 1930 it was decided to make the economic year coincide with the calendar year, so that the closing date of the Five-Year Plan was set at December 31, 1932. This precise date is not of great importance, because the experience of the first two years under the plan indicated that it would never be fulfilled as an organic whole on one date. Some processes, as will be shown in detail in the next chapter, leaped ahead so fast that within two years they passed the limits marked out in the original Five-Year Plan, and several industries give good promise of fulfilling the plan in three years. Side by side with these achievements difficulties and setbacks which the original plan did not at all foresee cropped up to make the execution of the scheme a matter of the most intense stress and strain.

Before proceeding to a detailed examination of the Five-Year Plan in practice, one may inquire why the Soviet Government decided to subject the economic life of the country to such a rigorous test. The Five-Year Plan may first of all, perhaps, be considered a declaration of economic independence, as against the outside world. This does not mean that the Soviet Union is aiming at a purely self-contained existence or that it proposes, after the completion of the plan or at any other time, to cut off business intercourse with foreign countries. On the contrary, every effort is being made to increase the Soviet Union's share in world trade. But the successful achievement of the Five-Year Plan will bring the Soviet Union closer to the goal of self-sufficiency as regards basic and essential products. It will give a tremendous impetus to the development of the machine-building, metal and chemical industries, which are so important in modern economic life. The difference between the Soviet economic and social systems and those which prevail in the rest of the world, combined with the repeatedly expressed conviction of Soviet and Communist leaders that some capitalist power or powers will some day launch an attack against the Soviet Union, makes the desire for the maximum measure of economic self-sufficiency quite understandable.

Ever since Great Britain broke off relations with the Soviet Union in the spring of 1927, Soviet leaders have been constantly proclaiming the existence of a more or less imminent " war menace " against their country. If apprehension as regards England has subsided, at least to some extent, since the Labor Government resumed diplomatic relations, Soviet suspicion has now transferred itself to France as the most probable enemy, and the spectacular trial of the self-confessed leaders of the Industrial Party in Moscow toward the end of 1930 was exploited as a means of showing alleged French espionage activities and plots for intervention.

That the Five-Year Plan will strengthen very considerably the military power of the Soviet Union is obvious. While facts and figures about the development of war industries are naturally not available in published form, it is unlikely that these industries are being neglected in the general expansion of production. Moreover, such plants as the Stalingrad tractor factory and the Nizhni Novgorod automobile works possess potential military as well as actual economic value. From the manufacture of tractors to the making of tanks is not an impossibly long step, and motor transport has long been recognized as one of the weak spots in the Soviet military machine. Another weak spot is the absence of facilities for manufacturing gases and countergases, and the sweeping development projected for the chemical industry seems calculated to eliminate this defect. An intensively developed iron and steel industry, under modern conditions, is also an essential prerequisite of military power. Many aspects of the Five-Year Plan are consequently closely linked up with the achievement of the Soviet objective of strengthening the defensive capacity of the country.

Finally, the plan is, as it is often called, " a program of socialist offensive." Its adoption sounded the death knell of the two main neo-capitalist classes which grew up under the early conditions of the Nep: the Nepmen, or private traders and merchants, in the towns, and the *kulaks* in the villages. The open and veiled expropriation which has overtaken both these classes during the first years of the plan indicates that in a not very distant future, barring some sweeping change of policy, the only traders of any consequence will be state and cooperative agents, while the formerly individualist peasant producers will be more and more brought under the regimented discipline of the collective farms.

CHAPTER II

THE FIVE–YEAR PLAN IN EXECUTION [1]

(a) The Growth of Industry

AT the time of writing (December, 1930) the Five-Year Plan has been in operation for a little more than two years. Many of its projects have not developed according to the original forecasts. In some cases the results already obtained and the prospective results of future years, as has been said above, considerably exceed the requirements of the plan. At the same time hardships and difficulties have developed which were not contemplated by the plan's framers. In view of the uneven course of Soviet economic development during the last two years

---

[1] The statistical data in this section are taken from a variety of Soviet sources, including *Pyatiletni Plan: Narodno-Khozyaistvennovo Stroyitelstva SSSR* (The Five-Year Plan of National Economic Construction of the Soviet Union), published by the Planned Economic Life publishing house; "The Year of Bolshevik Tempo," an article by A. Maimin, published in two parts in *Pravda* of October 24 and October 28, 1930; "The Year of Bolshevik Offensive," an article by G. Vizhnitzer, in *Izvestia* of November 4, 1930; and "Results of Two Years of The Five-Year Plan," a communication made by the President of the State Planning Commission, V. V. Kuibishev, to the American news agency, Associated Press, and published in *Izvestia* of December 4, 1930.

it seems advisable to discuss the Five-Year Plan from a number of aspects, leaving the problem of agriculture, on account of its preeminent and basic importance, for a separate chapter.

Measured by the standards of quantity output and capital building the requirements of the Five-Year Plan, in most branches of industry, have been exceeded during 1929 and 1930. Gross industrial production increased by about 24% in 1928–29 and by 25% in 1929–30, whereas the plan called for increases, in those years, of 21.4% and 21.5% respectively. Due to the change in reckoning the Soviet economic year from January to January instead of from October to October, the months of October, November and December, 1930, were regarded as constituting a special quarter, when production was to increase by 38.5%, as against the average output for the preceding year. A still steeper climb in production is envisaged for 1931, when the industrial output is supposed to exceed the output for 1930 by 45%, whereas the original calculation for the third year of the Five-Year Plan called for an increase by 22%.[1]

The Five-Year Plan projected an output to the

[1] Since the percentage increase is by compound progression the 1931 production is 240% of that of 1927.

value of 29,338,000,000 rubles for the first two years of its operation, while the actual value of the output during this time was 30,456,000,000 rubles.[1] Investments in industrial construction during the two years amounted to 4,605,000,000 rubles, as against a proposed figure of 3,990,000,000 rubles.

The increase of output above the planned figures has not been evenly distributed. The basic machine building, metal and fuel industries have done better than those industries which produce goods for everyday consumption. Thus, the growth of output of the former industries has been 24% above plan, while in the latter there has been a failure to keep up with the planned figures of growth by 4 or 5%.

This relative as well as absolute growth of the so-called heavy industries is illustrated by the fact that the percentage of the output of the heavy industries in the whole volume of industrial production has increased from 43 in 1927–28 to 46.8 in 1928–29 and 48 in 1929–30. In 1931 it is expected to reach 52%. By 1933 the Soviet Union expects to become the first country in Europe in the production of coal and pig iron. Practically

---

[1] The ruble in these computations is a fixed standard of value, so that there is no question of price fluctuations. Its theoretical par of exchange is $0.51455.

all the figures of industrial output designed for the last year of the *pyatiletka*, 1932–33, have been drastically revised upward, as may be seen from the following table published in *Izvestia*, of November 10, 1930:

TOTAL PRODUCTION IN 1932–33

	According to Five-Year Plan	*Actually Expected*
Coal	75,000,000 tons	130,000,000 tons
Oil	21,700,000 tons	41,000,000 tons
Coke	11,700,000 tons	20,000,000 tons
Peat	13,700,000 tons	33,000,000 tons
Pig Iron	10,000,000 tons	17,000,000 tons
Steel	10,400,000 tons	20,000,000 tons
Rolled	8,000,000 tons	15,000,000 tons
Copper	84,500 tons	265,000 tons
Cement	40,000,000 barrels	100,000,000 barrels
Bricks	6,000,000,000	26,000,000,000
Tractors	53,000	150,000
Automobiles	105,000	200,000
Electro-Technical Industry	896,000,000 rubles	4,260,000,000 rubles
Electrical Energy	22,000,000,000 kw.-hours	33,000,000,000 kw.-hours
General Machine building	2,100,000,000 rubles	6,000,000,000 rubles
Agricultural Machinery	610,000,000 rubles	2,000,000,000 rubles
Pairs of Shoes	80,000,000	190,000,000

It is now expected that the goals set by the Five-Year Plan, as regards industrial output, will in most cases be realized within four years, and in some cases in even shorter terms. If the program of expanding industrial production by 45% in 1931 is carried out, it is estimated that 98% of the Five-Year Plan, so far as the output of the heavy industries is concerned, and 79% as regards all industries will have been fulfilled. By the end of 1931 three and a quarter years will have elapsed since the beginning of the Five-Year Plan.

There are several reasons for this speeding up of a program which was originally regarded as highly strained and extremely ambitious.[1] The reorganization of agriculture on a collectivized and mechanized basis, described in another chapter, went very much faster than the Five-Year Plan had contemplated. The success of this reorganization depends in large degree upon the equipment of the new state and collective farms with tractors and other large agricultural machines. This, in turn, demands heightened standards of output from those industries which are most directly connected with tractor manufacture and operation — the steel and oil industries, for in-

---

[1] It should be borne in mind that in all these comparisons it is the maximum, not the minimum variation of the original Five-Year Plan that comes into account.

stance. And it is impossible to double the output of steel and oil without making corresponding upward readjustments in the estimates of output of coal, building materials, etc.

The practicability of these sweeping increases is defended on the ground that the original Five-Year Plan overlooked productive possibilities. Moreover, as will be described later, a number of special stimuli for intensifying the productivity of workers and plants have been devised under the stress of the national drive for high-speed industrialization.

No large country in the world can show a rate of quantitative industrial progress comparable with that of the Soviet Union during the last eight years. The annual percentages of increase in gross industrial output over the preceding year are as follows:[1]

[1] [The percentages are cumulative, and are not, therefore, comparative. Such a comparison is available from the Amtorg Trading Corporation on a slightly different percentage base than that given above:

	Annual Gain	Per Cent of 1921–22	Per Cent of 1913
1921–22		100	21.8
1922–23	45.8	145.8	30.0
1923–24	30.8	190.7	39.6
1924–25	63.0	310.9	62.5
1925–26	42.7	443.8	89.2
1926–27	17.2	520.1	104.5
1927–28	22.5	637.1	131.1
1928–29	23.7	788.1	162.5
1929–30	24.2	978.8	201.9

Editor.]

1922–23	31%	1926–27	14.5%
1923–24	32%	1927–28	21.6%
1924–25	55%	1928–29	24%
1925–26	45.2%	1929–30	25%
	1931	45% (Projected)	

While the high percentages of the early years are not so significant, in view of the low level to which Russian industry had declined after the civil war, it is noteworthy that since 1926–27, when the prewar level of output was reached, there has been a steady growth in the percentages of increase. The volume of Russian industrial output is now about double the prewar figure and will be almost treble the 1913 figures if the ambitious plan for 1931 is carried out.

In some of the more important individual industries a comparison of output for 1913, 1925–26 and 1929–30 yields the following results:

	1913	*1925–26*	*1929–30*
Kilowatts of Electrical Energy	1,945,000,000	3,240,000,000	8,000,000,000
Tons of Coal	28,900,000	25,400,000	45,700,000
Tons of Oil....	9,300,000	8,500,000	17,100,000
Tons of Pig Iron...........	4,210,000	2,220,000	5,000,000
Tons of Rolled Steel	3,500,000	2,200,000	4,500,000

Agricultural Machinery (Reckoned in prewar prices)........	67,000,000 rubles	70,000,000	312,000,000
Barrels of Cement..........	12,300,000	8,500,000	24,000,000

Much of the growth of industrial production in the Soviet Union is due not so much to the expansion of old industries as to the development of new lines of production which were either quite unknown or negligibly developed in prewar Russia. Among the new things which are being produced in the Soviet Union are tractors, automobiles, powerful turbines and generators, chemical apparatus, oil-drilling machinery and Diesel motors. The Soviet leather and match factories and a considerable part of the textile factories are supplied with Soviet machinery.

Among the most important of the new plants which have begun to function during the first two years of the *pyatiletka* are the Stalingrad tractor factory, the Rostov factory for the manufacture of agricultural machinery, a large paper factory near Nizhni Novgorod, oil refineries in Baku and Grozny, a mechanized sawmill in Archangel and several electrical stations. In 1927–28, 59 new

41

enterprises, built at a cost of 156,000,000 rubles, commenced to work; in 1929–30, 221 new plants, valued at 839,600,000 rubles, were opened. Despite this progress, the complaint is often heard that new construction under the Five-Year Plan is spread over too wide a field and consequently fails to yield effective results within a reasonable length of time. In 1931 an attempt will be made to concentrate efforts on finishing those enterprises which are most essential and which are nearing completion, instead of dissipating energy by starting the construction of a multitude of new plants.

At first sight there seems to be an inexplicable contradiction between the rapidly mounting figures of industrial production registered under the Five-Year Plan and the acute shortage of industrial products, which is equally obvious in daily life and in the functioning of the Soviet industries. The explanation of this contradiction does not, I think, lie in any fundamental unreliability of the figures which have been cited. Errors of detail are always possible, perhaps more possible in the Soviet Union than in some other countries; but it is simply inconceivable that the Soviet authorities should year after year publish deliberately falsified sets of statistics for the guidance of the work of the state industries.

The first thing to remember when one is bewildered by the effort to reconcile the figures indicating a doubling of the prewar production with the fact that many manufactured articles which could certainly easily have been bought in prewar times are now either unobtainable or obtainable only with the greatest difficulty, is that the lion's share of the increased production is represented by machinery, equipment, construction work, etc., which are not objects of everyday use.

Furthermore, the output even of those branches of industry which register the greatest gains is swallowed up with amazing rapidity in the general process of rapid industrialization. A quantity of coal, for instance, which might have far exceeded Russia's needs a few years ago may prove inadequate at a time when new factories and expanding railroad lines are constantly demanding more fuel. The same consideration holds good for steel, for electrical energy and for many other things. Industrial construction has the right of way over individual comfort in the Soviet Union; and one reason why there is such a shortage of bolts, hinges and many other humble metal articles is that the reserves of iron and steel are largely earmarked for the requirements of industry and transport.

Although the growth of industrial production last year exceeded the projects of the Five-Year Plan, it fell short of the heightened demands which were set at the beginning of the year. Instead of increasing by 32% output grew by 25%. The failure to fill out the enlarged plan was especially marked in the coal and metal, textile and sugar industries, both of the latter being handicapped by inadequate supplies of raw material. The failure was keenly reflected in the economic life of the country, factories which depended upon coal and metal often being delayed in their work while the population went on short rations of textiles and sugar (among many other things). This incident shows that when the Soviet industrial machine is being run at high speed, the least failure to realize the planned output in any branch of industry may have consequences out of all apparent proportion to the degree of the failure. The country's industries are working with extremely limited reserves of fuel and raw material and other supplies, and therefore the breakdown of any part of the plan sends reverberations through the whole economic structure.

A final and far from unimportant consideration, when one is trying to solve the perennial puzzle presented by the sweeping figures of industrial growth, combined with the obvious inability of supply to catch up with demand, is that a given quantity of goods in the Soviet Union does not necessarily represent the same effective value that it might in prewar Russia or in America or Western Europe to-day. This raises the problem of quality in industrial production, which deserves treatment in a separate section.

(b) The Problem of Quality

Quality is a broad term. Applied to Soviet industrial production it may have three applications: to the standards of workmanship maintained in manufacturing, to such elements in the production process as overhead costs and labor productivity, and to the technical efficiency displayed in the management of factories and mines, old and new. In none of these fields has the showing of Soviet industry under the Five-Year Plan been as favorable as it has been in the sphere of quantity output.

Low quality has always been the Achilles' heel of Soviet industrial production. Several years ago, when Leon Trotzky held a post in the Supreme Economic Council, he conceived the idea of setting up a department where quality of production could be tested. This department was soon overwhelmed with specimens of bad workmanship: knives that failed to cut, textile goods that tore at the slightest pressure, shoes that leaked.

The Soviet economic press for years has been urging an improvement in this field; but little, if any, visible success has been achieved. Two factors in keeping up standards of quality in other countries — competition and fear of loss in sales— have not been operative in the Soviet Union, where competition is excluded by the socialist economic system and the goods shortage has been so chronically acute that consumers have been glad to take what they could get. The Supreme Economic Council on January 6, 1930, issued an "Order No. 559" in which it threatened severe punitive measures, including even prosecution in the courts, against individuals who might be responsible for putting out goods of low quality. The organ of the Supreme Economic Council, *Za Industrializatsiyu*,[1] on January 8, 1930, summarized the situation in regard to quality of production in a leading article, part of which reads as follows:

The poor quality of production becomes a menacing obstacle for the growth of our economic life, and first of all for the growth of industry itself. In 1926–27 and 1927–28

[1] Subsequently referred by translated title, *For Industrialization*.

the quality of production was already unsatisfactory. The Party and the Government instructed industry to raise the quality of production; but instead of this industry not only didn't improve, but, on the other hand, in a number of cases worsened the quality of production. And on October 8, 1929, the presidium of the Supreme Economic Council was compelled to state, to the shame of our undertakings and trusts, that in a number of branches of industry a sharp deterioration of the quality of production was revealed in 1928–29.

The bonds which unite all branches of industry among themselves work with merciless logicality. The low quality of coke and coal is one of the basic causes of the breach on the front of southern metallurgy. The extremely bad quality of metal caused a nonfulfilment of the program of the metal manufacturing industry. The course of work of our agricultural machine building during the first quarter threatens the provision of the sowing campaign with agricultural machines, and here the lumber trusts are guilty in high degree because they did not furnish wood of the necessary quality. The bad quality of the products of light industry intensifies the goods famine on the market and reduces the real wages of the workers. Such a situation discredits the work of industry in the eyes of the whole country.

In the same newspaper of December 28, 1929, an article, signed by N. Vinogradsky, contains the statements that " with an established average of damaged goods of 4 to 7% the actual proportion of such goods exceeds 25% and often goes up to 50% and more," and that " the majority of the enumerated defects [in the quality of goods] have as a direct result the diminution of the durability of the goods."

The former head of the Supreme Economic Council, V. V. Kuibishev, in the course of his speech before the Communist Party Congress held in June and July, 1930, spoke of the abnormally high percentage of cinders in the coal output, estimating this percentage at 14 or 16 and suggesting that if some improvement were not made 6,000 trains in 1931 would be required to carry this useless and, indeed, harmful ingredient in the coal. The former Commissar for Transport, Y. E. Rudzutak, in a speech delivered shortly before the opening of the congress, referred to a case in which the Supreme Economic Council refused to guarantee for five years rails which in prewar times were expected to last 45 years.

That quality remained a weak spot in the Soviet productive process throughout 1930 may be inferred from a statement in *Izvestia* of November 3, 1930, to the effect that " if during the last year we achieved some successes in reducing costs of production and building, along the line of quality of production we obtained not improvement but further deterioration."

Inferior quality of output must therefore be regarded as an incalculable, but heavy, discounting factor in estimating the real effectiveness of the quantitative gains which have been registered in Soviet industry year after year. It is not improbable that in some cases, at least, quality is sacrificed to quantity. The Five-Year Plan of setting so many high statistical goals has weaknesses as well as advantages. It creates a strong temptation to neglect those aspects of production which, like quality, are not susceptible of precise statistical definition. If, for example, a manager of a state factory is instructed to turn out more goods than his supplies of raw material would warrant he is under a certain pressure to produce the required number of goods by lessening the amount of raw material used, to the consequent detriment of the quality of his output. A failure to realize the quantitative task which he has been set will almost certainly lead to censure and punishment; poor quality is less easy to detect and more likely to go unnoticed, in view of its widespread prevalence.

To a certain extent there has been an effort to establish "qualitative indices " for industry. The control figures for each year include such items as costs of production and labor productivity. In this field, in contrast to the figures of quantity output, where the plan has been consistently exceeded during the last three years, there has been a record of almost continuous failure to reach the goals which were set, even though some reduction in production costs has been achieved and labor productivity has grown, in connection with the introduction of more modern machinery and equipment. The percentages of reduction aimed at and achieved during the last few years are as follows:

	Aim	*Achievement*
1925–26	5%	Increase by 1.17%
1926–27	5%	Decrease by 1.8%
1927–28	6.3%	Decrease by 6.2%
1928–29	7%	Decrease by 4.2%
1929–30	11%	Decrease by 7%

It was planned to increase labor productivity by 25% during 1929–30; but the actual increase was only about half that figure. Failure to carry out fully the plans of increasing productivity and reducing costs, as will be shown later, was a serious factor in causing financial difficulties during the last year.

There is much room for improvement in the efficiency of the management of the Soviet factories. Several gloomy accounts of operating difficulties in the new Stalingrad tractor plant have appeared in the Soviet newspapers. One of these, which was printed in *For Industrialization* of November 20, 1930, accuses the manager of the factory of preparing an excessive production program " without any account of the possibilities of an unequipped and still unprepared enterprise." The account, which is quite long and detailed, mentions a case where, as a result of the impatience and technical unwisdom of the manager, the conveyor was pushed ahead when it was unfit for use, with the result that it broke down and required extensive repairs. Other machinery was broken and the production program of the factory was carried out only in very small percentages. " Instead of soberly considering, immediately recognizing his exaggeration, promptly working out actual productive possibilities, making up a precise plan and proceeding to organize production and administration, the director preferred administrative terror as a means of guidance. He lacked the civic courage to recognize his mistakes."

Similar undesirable developments occurred at a new glass factory which was built in the village of Belaya Bichka. Two correspondents in *For Industrialization* of November 22 submitted a report on this plant, from which we may take the following salient excerpts:

51

In the construction of this huge glass plant there were so many mistakes and omissions that in this respect it must become a model of improper construction and builders must learn from it how not to build. . . . The fundamental question of a fuel and raw material base was not solved up to this time. The first information about sand on the territory of the plant was unfounded and as a result it is necessary to bring sand from a railroad station 380 kilometers distant from the factory. . . . The factory is a model of unprojected building; for three years it was built without any project. . . . Estimates of the cost of the plant continually changed and grew from 1,016,000 rubles to 11,647,000 rubles. As a result of the chaotic character of the accounting it is impossible precisely to establish the cost of the plant.

No doubt most industrial undertakings in the Soviet Union operate more satisfactorily than the examples which have just been cited would indicate. It is often necessary in other countries to pay heavily for first experiences in initiating a new form of production, as is tractor manufacturing in the Soviet Union. But although quality is not a thing that can be measured very adequately in a statistical sense, there can be little doubt that failures in this field at least partially nullify some of the striking quantitative gains which have been described and which furnish part of the answer to the perpetual paradox of Soviet economics: the failure of supply to keep pace with demand, notwithstanding the extraordinary percentages of increase in industrial output which are announced from year to year.

(c) Wages, Labor and Living Standards

During the first two years of its operation the Five-Year Plan demanded sacrifices in the living standards of the population which were not in any way contemplated or foreseen in the original draft of the project. One can find in this draft not only general estimates to the effect that real wages must increase faster than nominal wages because of the declining cost of living, but also exact calculations of how much more meat and milk people will consume when the Five-Year Plan is completed.

Money wages in the Soviet industries have advanced steadily, both before and after the adoption of the Five-Year Plan. Thus, the average monthly wage in all Soviet industries increased from 60.38 rubles in 1926–27 to 66.90 rubles in 1927–28, to 73.35 rubles in 1928–29 and to 76.22 rubles in 1929–30.[1]

But the real purchasing power of the ruble declined heavily between 1928 and 1930. This decline was expressed not in a general rise in the

[1] See "Problems of Labor in Figures," a publication of the Soviet Commissariat for Labor, p. 59–61.

53

price level, because the prices of staple necessities were held fairly stable in the state and cooperative stores, but in the vanishing of many articles from these stores and in the sharp contraction of the quantity of many others which might be bought. Rationing was discarded along with military communism. Between 1922 and 1928 one could use a Soviet ruble very much as one could use a dollar, a pound or a mark; it was possible to go into a store and buy whatever was offered for sale. True, one could not be sure of finding a well-stocked shop: beginning with 1925 a goods shortage began to be felt, especially in the country districts; and failure of the state industries to produce textiles, boots, clothing and other articles of general consumption fast enough to keep up with the peasant demand was not the least of the factors which caused the peasants to hold back their grain from sale. There were occasional periods of scarcity in the supply of individual commodities, such as butter and lemons. But in general the supplying of the population with food and manufactured goods proceeded without special limitations or restrictions.

Beginning with 1928 a shortage of bread began to manifest itself and rationed sale of bread was introduced in some provincial towns. In 1929 this practice became universal, so far as the sale of bread in the towns was concerned, and a number of other foodstuffs went on the rationed list: sugar, meat, butter, macaroni, eggs, etc. By 1930 the shortage had extended even to candies and cigarettes. By the end of 1930 potatoes were almost the only important article of food which was not rationed.

Rationing in the Soviet Union applies only to sales in state and cooperative stores. There is a small and precarious private market where things may be bought in unrestricted quantities. But in this private market, where the law of supply and demand works unchecked, prices are so fantastically high as to exclude any possibility of extensive buying by people whose incomes, even measured in paper rubles, are far from high. Butter, for instance, has averaged about seven rubles (nominally $3.50) a pound on the Moscow free market; meat has commanded three or four rubles a pound. A visit to the Sukharevka, Moscow's chief private market for goods, in the summer of 1930 revealed prices of from 35 to 60 rubles for shoes and from 100 to 150 rubles for boots, while a small bar of inferior chocolate was priced at a ruble and a half.

If one compares these prices with incomes,

which in Moscow may average 100 rubles per month for workers and 150 for employees, it is obvious that a visit to the free market is a luxury which cannot be repeated very often. The prices of rationed commodities vary, as a rule, from a third to a sixth of the free market prices. It would be difficult, if not impossible, to state precisely what the Russian consumer is able to obtain under the rationing system, because the ration allotments vary from time to time and children and manual workers receive preference over other classes of the population.

Generally speaking, in Moscow (which is rather better taken care of than the average provincial town by the central supplying agencies, although prices on its free markets are somewhat higher, as a rule, than prices on markets in smaller towns which are closer to sources of agricultural products) amounts obtainable on the food booklets which are given to all citizens who enjoy political rights were as follows:

Manual workers obtained two pounds of bread a day and other consumers one pound. Manual workers received 200 grams (a little less than half a pound) of meat a day, as against 100 grams for other holders of food booklets.[1] The general

---

[1] There are ten or twelve meatless days every month.

sugar allotment was one and a half kilograms (3.3 pounds) a month. Eggs were not sold to ordinary consumers; if workers or children received them, the limit was five eggs a month. A similar situation prevailed with butter, of which the favored classes of consumers might receive every month half or, at the most, three quarters of a pound; many people were obliged to do without it altogether, unless they could afford to pay the inflated prices of the free market. In the winter of 1930–31 there was some effort to provide margarine as a substitute for butter, but also in very limited quantities. During the first part of 1930 children below the age of twelve were permitted to buy half a liter of milk a day at the comparatively moderate price of 24 kopeks a liter; later in the year the sale of milk in cooperative stores ceased almost entirely, while the price of milk on the free market leaped from 60 kopeks to a ruble and a half a liter. Other food allotments which held good for Moscow over a considerable part of the year were 600 grams of grits, 200 grams of macaroni and 50 grams of tea per month. Children were given some preferential supplies of rice and cereals.

The supply of fruit and vegetables, with the exception of cabbage and potatoes, was scarce and irregular. Although there was a good crop of vegetables last summer, extremely faulty methods of transportation and distribution caused the loss of a considerable part of the produce through spoiling before it could reach the consumers. The staple diet of the average Russian family during the latter part of 1930 consisted of cabbage, potatoes, bread, herring, grits (the rough Russian cereal known as *kasha*) and tea. The shortage of meat, milk and dairy products and fats was most keenly felt in the latter part of 1930, and an inconvenient shortage of soap was caused by the lack of animal fats. Such ordinary articles of diet as cheese and sausage were apparently regarded as luxuries and were placed on sale in special state shops at 15 or 20 rubles a kilogram.

The reduction in the Soviet standard of living during the first years of the Five-Year Plan has not affected all classes equally. Special efforts have been made to relieve the situation of the manual workers by organizing factory restaurants and introducing a system under which stores are attached to factories, so that only workers in the latter may buy there. It is held that this measure tends to reduce the formidable amount of standing in line for products which is so characteristic of contemporary Soviet life, and to insure the principle of " class supply " by giving the workers preference with food and goods. Even when one takes full account of these factors, however, it does not seem that the workers' standard of living under the rationing restrictions, despite the increase in their money wages, was equal to that which prevailed in the later years of the Nep, from 1925 until 1927. The reduction in the living standards of less favored classes has been greater and has been greatest of all, naturally, with the disfranchised classes, who are denied the benefit of food booklets.

What causes have brought about the food stringency in the Soviet Union, which has always been a rich agricultural country? In the writer's opinion there are four, which may be listed in the order of relative importance as follows:

(1) The agrarian revolution (described in a separate chapter), which destroyed the surplus production of the richer peasants in many food-stuffs faster than it created new reserves of surplus produce through the state and collective farms.

(2) The rapid increase in the demand for food, connected with the growth of the cities and the necessity for provisioning millions of new wage earners, employed in industrial plants and construction projects.

59

(3) The frequently unsatisfactory functioning of transportation and of the cooperative distributive system. The wastage of perishable food products through delayed transportation and improper storage has in some cases been little short of appalling.

(4) The exportation of such food products as eggs, butter, fruit, caviar and preserves. This sacrifice was demanded of the population because of the imperative need of realizing foreign currency to pay for the machinery and equipment needed for the realization of the projects of industrialization.[1] The dimensions of this export, however, were comparatively small and its total elimination would by no means have solved the food problem.

If the causes of food shortage are thus fairly clear, it is somewhat more difficult to understand the acute lack of many manufactured products, especially in the light of the phenomenal figures of quantitative growth which the Soviet industries have been revealing over a period of years. Yet this lack is one of the most obvious features of contemporary Soviet life. Stores are fairly mobbed when some shoddy clothing or shoes are offered for sale. There is an extraordinary shortage of the simplest articles of daily use—" pri-

---

[1] Exported wheat was deemed to be surplus.

muses," or oil-stoves, on which the Russians do most of their cooking, bolts, nails, brooms, etc.

Here again one may perhaps suggest four factors which help to explain Russia's chronic crisis of disproportion between supply and demand, a crisis, which, it may be noted, is precisely the reverse of the one which has recently affected the countries of Western Europe and America so severely. In those countries there are recurring periods of depression when effective demand does not keep up with supply; the Soviet economic problem is to bring supply up to a point where it can satisfy demand. The four important contributing causes of the goods shortage may be stated as follows:

(1) The lion's share in the 20 and 25% increases of industrial production during recent years has fallen to the so-called heavy industries, which do not produce goods for everyday use.

(2) The element of poor quality, described in the preceding section, shortens the life of the goods and consequently lowers the real effectiveness of the numerical figures of their output.

(3) The practically complete cessation of all imports which do not fall under such categories as machinery, equipment and indispensable raw material, creates many hardships and inconveniences,

because the Soviet Union is far from being a self-sufficing producer of articles of general use.

(4) Consuming demand grows very rapidly, perhaps more rapidly than the output of the "light" industries, which turn out goods for immediate consumption. This is because the money wage payments of the industries constantly increase, on account of the hiring of new workers and employees, and of the raising of the nominal wage level from year to year, while the new system of collectivized agriculture tends to increase the money earnings of the poorer peasants.

When the country will emerge from its crisis of inadequate supply is a doubtful problem. Communist economists see a turn of the tide already, in view of the fact that there was a substantial increase in the output of grain, cotton and sugar-beets in the state and collective farms in 1930. They foresee a solution of the food shortage in the organization of a number of large state cattle ranches, and pig, poultry and dairy farms.

An important economic change which occurred in 1930, and which Soviet advocates were not slow to greet as a proof of the superiority of their economic system over "capitalism," was the disappearance of nonpolitical unemployment. This qualification is essential, because members of disfranchised classes (priests and ministers of religion, merchants, traders, former aristocrats, *kulaks*, or formerly well-to-do peasants, etc.) and of their families are, as a rule, barred from public employment in the Soviet Union. Apart from these classes the Soviet Union until 1930 had a considerable figure of registered unemployment, which varied as a result of seasonal and other causes, but never fell below 1,000,000 and sometimes approached 2,000,000.

During 1930, however, this reserve of registered unemployed disappeared and a definite shortage of labor made itself felt in some of the rougher and less desirable fields of labor: lumbering, coal mining, freight loading, labor on new construction projects, etc. In October, 1930, payment of unemployment benefit was definitely stopped, except to persons who could prove ill health, and the labor exchanges were instructed to send applicants immediately to work. The network of institutions for training unskilled labor was extended.

At the same time stricter measures were adopted against the migratory tendencies of some of the industrial workers, which led to a high labor turnover and consequent diminution of efficiency. During the summer months of 1930, for instance, 50,000 miners left the Donetz Basin, partly repelled by the difficult living conditions there and partly attracted by the unusually good harvest in the Ukrainian villages from which many of them had originally come. The result was a disastrous fall in the output of coal and a failure to realize the year's production program in the coal industry.

Now, persons who leave work without adequate cause may not be sent to another post in industry or transport for a period of six months, but during this time may be employed only on rough, unskilled labor. Persistent " deserters from the labor front " may be expelled from their trade unions, which involves a loss of most valuable privileges as regards food supply and other things. There is a movement to persuade workers to pledge themselves to remain at their present posts until the end of the Five-Year Plan. Engineers and other specialists who without permission leave the posts to which they have been assigned have in some cases been formally prosecuted in the courts and sent back to their posts by legal sentence.

Two main causes, high-speed industrialization and the collectivization of agriculture, account for the replacement of unemployment by labor shortage in Russia. There has been a steady and increasing growth in the number of employed wage-earners. In 1926–27 there were 2,365,000 workers in the large industries and 10,990,000 employed wage-earners altogether in the Soviet Union. By 1930 these figures had increased, respectively, to 3,557,000 and 13,684,000. In 1931 the number of industrial workers is expected to rise to 4,241,000 and the total number of wage-earners to 16,200,000.[1]

For some years prior to 1930 the increase in the number of workers was offset by a continual inflow of peasants, seeking work, into the towns. The poorer peasants were driven by economic necessity to supplement the scanty incomes from their land holdings with additional earnings as casual laborers in the towns. Moreover, there was the tendency to quit the country for the city which has been visible in many countries. The life of the city worker, with its limited hours, with the guaranteed social benefits and opportunities for recreation which the worker enjoys under the Soviet system, was an object of envy to the peasants.

But in 1930, when the need for more workers was greatest, the normal migration of peasants into the cities was substantially checked. The

[1] See article by the Soviet Commissar for Labor, A. Tsikhon, in *Izvestia*, for January 4, 1931.

new collective farms gave the poorer peasants an assured income and source of food supply. At the same time living conditions in the towns, due to the food shortage which has been described, became considerably less attractive. So the problem of recruiting and training new workers has become one of the most important of those which confront the Soviet economic authorities during the coming year.

(d) New Socialist Stimuli in Production

The Five-Year Plan has brought with it new socialist stimuli in production and a strenuous effort to transform the psychology of the Soviet worker in the sense of imbuing him with a stronger consciousness of personal interest in, and responsibility for, the success of the undertaking in which he is employed. The Soviet system, which is avowedly a dictatorship of the proletariat, or industrial working class, has always endeavored to appeal to the workers on the ground that the fruits of their labor are realized directly by themselves and do not go for the enrichment of an employing class.

The increased emphasis in this direction during the last two years has been strong and unmistakable. During the early years of the Nep the incentive of personal gain was to a large extent restored, even for workers in state industries. Wages were paid in accordance with the amount and value of work performed. While the Soviet trade unions were always under Communist leadership and never pushed their differences with the state trusts to the point of calling large scale strikes, they did to a considerable extent concentrate their attention upon securing for their members the rights to which they were entitled under the collective agreements which, together with the labor laws, governed wages and working conditions in Soviet industries. The idea that the trade unions should also take an active part in spurring the workers on to higher productivity was allowed to fall into the background. Now, however, this idea has been placed prominently in the foreground and the elimination of Mikhail Tomsky as president of the Trade Union Council and of Nikolai Uglanov as Commissar for Labor may be interpreted as a sign that the tendency, stigmatized as "right wing" or "opportunist," to place the emphasis upon care for the material interests of the trade union members, rather than upon the function of the trade unions as organizers and pacemakers in stimulating production, has been abandoned by the Communist Party leadership.

Some special effort to press into service psychological as well as purely material inducements was probably necessary in view of the fact that the heightened labor productivity required under the Five-Year Plan coincided with a time of considerable hardship as regards the supply of food and manufactured goods. Among the more important of the new socialist stimuli to production which are now widely applied in factories and, perhaps to a lesser extent, in offices, state and collective farms and even in universities throughout the Soviet Union the following may be mentioned: (1) Socialist competition; (2) Shock brigades; (3) Conveyor brigades; (4) " Public towing;" (5) Extra industrial financial plan; (6) Self-mobilization.

(1) Socialist competition is carried on between two or more factories, which are usually in the same branch of industry and are similar in size and production problems. The representatives of the competing factories draw up a formal agreement, each side pledging itself to fulfill certain concrete tasks in such fields as reduction of costs, more rational use of fuel and raw material, and improvement of the quality of the finished product. The signing of these contracts is accompanied by much speechmaking and is generally made as impressive

as possible with a view to arousing the interest, enthusiasm and local pride of the workers, on whom the carrying out of the proposed improvements depends.

(2) Shock brigades are groups of workers who undertake to exceed the normal requirements of output. If necessary they work on evenings and on free days. They study and suggest methods by which the factory production can be advanced. Inasmuch as the piecework system is widely practiced in Soviet factories, the activities of these brigades often lead to an increase in the amount of work which is done for a given rate of pay.

(3) " Conveyor brigades " are a variation and extension of the shock brigades system. This name is applied to a system under which a piece of work is carried through one department after another by picked groups in each department who make themselves responsible for its speedy execution.

(4) " Public towing " is a peculiar nautical phrase which is employed when a plant which has been fulfilling its program well assumes a sort of informal guardianship over one that has been lagging behind. Workers from the former plant go to the latter, offer suggestions from their own experience and generally endeavor to raise morale.

(5) The extra industrial financial plan reflects the effort which each factory and collective farm is supposed to make to outstrip the production figures which have been assigned to it, without increasing cost or lowering quality. The deposed All-Russian Premier, S. I. Sirtsov, attacked this experiment on the ground that it imposed an undue strain upon the workers; but one of the defendants in the trial of the self-confessed members of the " Industrial Party " gladdened the hearts of the Communists by testifying that the initiative of the workers in the factories, expressed in this extra plan, had defeated all the efforts of sabotaging engineers to hold down production.

(6) " Self-mobilization " has been adopted as a means of combatting the prevalent labor shortage without resorting to formal labor conscription. Such a measure would furnish additional material for foreign agitation against Russian exports as products of forced labor. Therefore, there is an effort to solve the problem by bringing various forms of inducement and pressure on workers, engineers and trained specialists of all kinds to declare themselves "self-mobilized " and pledged to remain at their posts until the Five-Year Plan is accomplished.

Model members of shock brigades are praised

and held up to public admiration and receive more tangible rewards in the shape of preferential supply with food and clothing, first consideration when places are allotted in rest homes and sanatoria, promotion to more responsible posts, etc. Through socialist competition, shock brigades and similar devices, the Soviet régime is attempting to extract from the workers the very thing that often excites the resistance of trade unions in other countries—an increase of labor productivity in excess of the increase in money wages.[1]

The Soviet argument in this connection is, of course, that in its territory the workers are laboring for themselves and not for the profit of a private employer. In some cases this argument, driven home by the greatest propaganda machine in history, which the Soviet Government has at its disposal, finds acceptance; in other cases there is antagonism between the pace-making *udarniki*, as the members of the shock brigades are called, and those workers who resent the idea of being speeded up. Of course, in the event of conflict the potent resources of the Communist Party and the Soviet state apparatus are on the side of the *udarniki*.

---

[1] The " control figures " for 1931 prescribe a growth of labor productivity by 28%, a growth of wages by 6% in industry and by 8% in transport.

Lenin more than once expressed the view that the issue between " capitalism " and " socialism " would be settled, in the long run, by superior capacity for production. The means of arousing productive enthusiasm and strengthening labor discipline which have been outlined represent an attempt to furnish socialist substitutes for the familiar incentive of private self-enrichment which, although not altogether destroyed, is greatly weakened by the latest developments of Soviet economic policy. Some time must elapse before the efficacy of these substitutes can be judged, especially as they are very new, while the instinct of self-enrichment is, among other considerations, very old.

(e) Foreign Trade, Concessions and Technical Aid

Foreign trade is a vital link in the Soviet economic system because, in view of the absence of foreign loans or investments of capital, trade remains Russia's overwhelmingly most important means of paying for the foreign machinery, equipment and raw materials which are essential to the ambitious schemes of industrial development contemplated under the Five-Year Plan. It lends itself to planning with more difficulty than some other branches of economic life, because markets and prices are, to a large extent, outside Soviet control. Foreign trade has revived more slowly than industry, agriculture or transport. Soviet exports in 1928–29 were valued at 877,596,000 rubles and imports amounted to 836,303,000 rubles. The corresponding figures for 1913 were 1,520,000,000 rubles and 1,374,000,000 rubles.[1] Complete figures for 1929–30 are not available at the time of writing,[2] but statistics for the first nine months reveal exports of 726,901,000 rubles, as against imports of 803,275,000 rubles. The exports increased by a little over 100,000,000 rubles, as against the corresponding period in the previous year, while the imports increased by over 200,000,000 rubles.

The slow recovery of the Soviet export trade is largely due to the fact that the organization of Russian agriculture in the first decade after the Revolution was not calculated to yield a large export surplus. The large estates of the pre-

[1] *Soviet Union Year Book*, 1930, p. 289.

[2] These figures, when published, revealed imports to the value of 1,068,742,000 rubles, as against exports of 1,002,270,000 rubles. The gain in the total value of Soviet exports was due almost entirely to the re-emergence of the country as an exporter of grain. The two and a quarter million tons of grain which were shipped abroad up to October 1, 1930, realized about 120,000,000 rubles, and this sum almost exactly represented the gain in export value over 1928–29. While the volume of Soviet exports increased almost 50% the world decline in prices prevented a corresponding increase in value. The increase in the value of imports, which created an unfavorable trade balance of about 66,000,000 rubles, may be chiefly attributed to increased purchases of tractors, agricultural and industrial machinery, metal and metal products.

revolutionary landlords were completely destroyed, the land was divided among many peasant small holdings, and the farms of the prewar well-to-do peasants, the so-called *kulaks*, while not so completely annihilated before 1930 as the landlords' estates, were considerably reduced in size and productive capacity. The landlords and *kulaks* were the main producers for the export market, and their disappearance or decline left a gaping hole in such formerly important items of Russian export as wheat, barley, rye, flax, butter and eggs.

A few comparative figures illustrate this point. In 1913 Russian exports of wheat, barley and rye were valued at 441,100,000 rubles, whereas in 1928–29 such exports were absolutely negligible. Butter, eggs and flax shipped abroad in 1913 brought in respectively 71,159,000; 90,639,000 and 94,158,000 rubles, whereas the corresponding figures for 1928–29 were 33,713,000; 27,763,000 and 28,989,000 rubles. Increases in such products as oil, which yielded 132,614,000 rubles in 1928–29, as against 48,507,000 rubles in 1913, and furs, which amounted to 109,119,000 rubles in 1928–29 from 52,995,000 rubles in 1913, did not offset the heavy decline in the exports of agricultural produce. The Soviet Government is convinced that through the combined mechanization and collectivization of agriculture (described in the following chapter) it can regain Russia's old position as an exporter of agricultural products; and some basis for this belief may be found in the fact that in 1930, the first year of widespread collectivization, it was found possible, after an interval of four years, to resume grain exports on a tolerably substantial scale, although a huge gap in domestic consumption must be bridged before there will be a real basis for large scale exportation of meat and dairy products.

The world economic depression was a severe blow to the Soviet export plan for 1929–30, which called for the shipment abroad of goods to the value of 1,200,000,000 rubles. Although final figures have not been published, it is almost certain that this sum was not realized, largely because the fall in prices was felt with special severity in many of the articles which Russia exports. For the first nine months of 1929–30, although the volume of Soviet exports increased by 57%, the amount of money realized for them increased only by 17%. The situation in regard to the Soviet foreign trade balance was made more difficult because prices of equipment and machinery, which constitute about two thirds of the Soviet imports, did not fall as fast and as far as the prices of such Soviet exports as grain, fur and lumber. It is estimated that the Soviet Union lost about 30% on the prices of its exports, while it gained only about 15% through price reductions in its imports.

This combination of circumstances led to the ruthless stripping of the country of all articles available for export and ultimately led to charges by groups of producers, who felt the competition of the Soviet exports, that the Soviet Union was " dumping " its goods for the purpose of disorganizing world markets and promoting unemployment and discontent, with the ultimate aim of revolution. France adopted a license system in regard to Soviet exports; and conferences held by some of the agrarian states of Eastern Europe in Warsaw and Bukharest were interpreted in the Soviet Union as preparations for a united economic front against Soviet grain exports.

The Soviet Commissariat for Trade, in response to the French action, in the autumn of 1930 instructed Soviet commercial representatives abroad to refrain from placing orders in countries which discriminated against Soviet exports, or at least to reduce such orders to a minimum and to avoid, so far as possible, the chartering of ships or the utilization of other services in such countries.

Trade between the Soviet Union and France is so inconsiderable that neither the tariff restrictions nor the Soviet counter measures are likely to produce any great economic effect. The Soviet measures may, however, be regarded as a warning to other countries which have developed larger trade balances with the Soviet Union, such as the United States, Great Britain and Germany, that the Soviet Union will, so far as possible, cut down its purchases in countries which boycott or restrict its exports.

The Soviet case against the charge of dumping was stated by Assistant Commissar for Trade A. P. Rosenholtz (subsequently nominated Commissar for Foreign Trade when the Commissariat for Trade was divided into two sections) in the course of a press interview, published in *Izvestia* of October 22, 1930. After pointing out that the Soviet Union's grain exports had still not reached a third part of the prewar volume and contrasting its present share of 7 or 8% in the world export of wheat with the prewar share of 25%, Mr. Rosenholtz declared that the prolonged fall in world grain prices was due far more to the increased production of the United States, Argentina and Canada than to the Soviet's reappearance on the world grain market. After citing a statement in a French economic bulletin to show that southeastern European countries sometimes undersold Russia in the grain markets, Mr. Rosenholtz employed a familiar Soviet argument against restrictions on Russian export, saying:

At the present time there are branches of industry in some western countries which are working, for the most part, on Soviet orders. The disappearance of the latter could cause the complete closing or the partial shutting down of very big factories and of whole branches of industry, with a corresponding increase of unemployment. Is this a means of healing or mitigating the crisis? And it is not even necessary to prove that no country can develop its imports without exports, least of all the Soviet Union, which has no large credits.

It is just in this absence of large credits, rather than in any Machiavellian scheme to upset world economic life, that the explanation of the forced Soviet exports at low prices must be found. In view of the fact that every dollar of foreign currency is urgently needed for the more successful and speedier realization of the Five-Year Plan, on which the Soviet Government has staked its political and economic future, it is most unlikely that Soviet commercial organizations would deliberately accept lower prices for their goods than they could otherwise obtain, especially if one takes into account that the Soviet Union, which has in the neighborhood of two per cent of the world's trade, could not exert any very decisive influence on international market and price trends.

When one endeavors to investigate the correctness of the " dumping " charge one immediately encounters an almost unsurmountable obstacle in the shape of the fact that Soviet currency has no international value. It would not be difficult to show that many articles exported from the Soviet Union are sold abroad at prices considerably lower than those which prevail on the domestic market, — if one accepts the official valuation of the ruble at 1.94 to the dollar. But in reality a dollar may be worth enormously more to the Soviet Government than 1.94 rubles, or indeed, any specified number of rubles, which can be printed at will. Suppose that $10,000,000 worth of American tractors are urgently needed for Soviet state farms. Twenty million rubles will not buy these tractors; neither, for that matter, will 200,000,000 rubles. The tractors can be bought only with dollars or with some other stable foreign currency.

In view of this situation, Soviet export has been forced in the past, regardless both of the hardships entailed for the population and of the agitation which has been aroused in some foreign commercial circles; and there is every probability that it will continue to be forced in the future. There is little reason to believe that the Soviet Union, except in certain more or less localized Near and Middle Eastern markets, will figure prominently as an exporter of manufactured goods for many years to come. The quality of the Soviet goods is still, as a rule, too low, and there is an enormous, hungry internal market to be satisfied. But Soviet oil, lumber, grain, manganese and various other mineral and raw material commodities will be poured on the foreign markets in increasing quantities in future years, unless an absolute saturation point is reached or insuperable tariff barriers are erected against them.

The hardships of the Five-Year Plan have been intensified because the Soviet Union has been obliged to carry out its industrialization thus far without the aid of foreign capital. The Soviet Government has obtained no foreign loans; and the attempt to attract large scale investment of foreign capital through the granting of concessions, or leases for the operation of industrial, mining and other enterprises has not brought results. The only two concessions which involved an investment running into many millions of dollars were the W. A. Harriman concession for the exploitation of the manganese mines of the Chia-touri district, in the Caucasus, and the Lena Goldfields concession to an English corporation for the exploitation and development of gold, iron, copper, lead and zinc mines in specified districts of Siberia and the Urals. Both these agreements were signed in the spring of 1925, when Soviet internal policy was less uncompromisingly anti-"capitalist" than it became after the adoption of the Five-Year Plan. Both concessions ended unsuccessfully, the Harriman enterprise proving unprofitable to the concessionaire and being terminated by mutual agreement in 1928, although it was originally supposed to run for 20 years. The Lena Goldfields corporation ceased to operate its properties in the spring of 1930, and a barrage of mutual recriminations developed between the concessionaire and the Soviet Concessions Committee regarding the responsibility for the breakdown of this enterprise. While a number of concession enterprises are still functioning in Russia, they are not of great economic importance and their total output is less than a fraction of 1% of the total industrial production of the country. No new concession agreement was signed during 1930.[1]

[1] The last statement is made on the authority of the Main Concessions Committee.

Unable to attract foreign capital the Soviet Government, especially during recent years, has followed the policy of engaging the services of foreign engineering firms and of individual specialists and groups of specialists. A hundred and fifteen foreign firms were operating in the Soviet Union on these so-called technical aid contracts in the latter part of 1930. Germany and the United States were far in the lead in this form of activity, German firms holding 46 of the contracts and American firms 44.[1] About 2,000 American industrial and agricultural experts, engineers and mechanics, and probably about the same number of Germans were employed in Soviet territory in this connection.

The technical aid contract involves no investment of capital on the part of the foreign firm, which, on the contrary, is paid for its advice and engineering help.[2] Sometimes this arrangement is linked up to a certain extent with a sales agreement. For instance, the American General Electric Company in the autumn of 1928 sold to the Soviet Union $26,000,000 worth of electrical equipment on a long-term credit basis. Following this sale the General Electric Company sent a

[1] Data communicated personally to the author by the Foreign Department of the Supreme Economic Council.

[2] For list as of August 15, 1929, see *The Soviet Union Looks Ahead*, p. 273.

number of its engineers to Russia to supervise the installation of the equipment and render general technical assistance to the Soviet electrical industry. Somewhat similar arrangements were made in connection with Henry Ford's agreement to furnish technical aid for the new automobile plant which is being built in Nizhni Novgorod.

In other cases the rôle of the American firm has been of a purely advisory character. Albert Kahn Inc. of Detroit drew up the plans of the huge tractor plants, one of which has been built in Stalingrad, while another is in process of building in Cheliabinsk. It has also established in Moscow a bureau of engineers and draughtsmen, which is designing other new industrial plants. Arthur G. McKee & Co. of Cleveland is working on the huge Magnitogorsk steel plant in the Urals. Colonel Hugh L. Cooper, hydroelectric engineer, is chief consultant for the largest of the new Soviet hydroelectric power plants, Dnieprstroi, on the lower reaches of the River Dnieper. The list might be prolonged almost indefinitely.

There is scarcely any corner of the Soviet Union where one is not apt to encounter one or more of these American technical pioneers. Engineers trained in the mining camps of the West are employed in the copper mines of the Caucasus and Central Asia. An American irrigation expert, Arthur Powell Davis, with headquarters in Tashkent, is chief consultant on huge irrigation projects in Turkestan. Around the Stalingrad tractor factory is a whole colony of some 300 American mechanics, who are supposed to instruct the Russian workers in the processes of tractor production. American agricultural experts and tractor mechanics are scattered among the new large state farms.

In short, the American engineer and technician, usually indifferent to the Soviet political philosophy, but with a professional pride in doing a good job, has become an important, if not an indispensable, cog in the machine of Soviet industrialization. The Soviet Government feels that the money spent in engaging foreign specialists represents a good investment, both because these men can impart special instruction in branches of industry which were sometimes undeveloped in prewar Russia and because the American or West European engineer usually introduces a faster pace of work and more efficient methods. Not the least of the factors which will determine the ultimate success of the Five-Year Plan and of the general Soviet scheme of industrialization is the efficiency which the Russians will display in operating the plants which foreigners have to so large a degree designed for them.

(f) The Reconstruction of Transport

One of the things that make life so difficult and so strenuous under the Five-Year Plan is the proved difficulty of making every branch of industry keep in step when all are being pushed forward at such a giddy pace. In Soviet economic life there are always some of what the Russians call "narrow places" — i. e., insufficiently developed branches which hold back the advance of the others. One of the narrowest of these "narrow places" at the present time is the transportation system of the country, the reconstruction of which, as Stalin declared at the Communist Party Congress in the summer of 1930, "lags behind the general tempo of development." Inadequate transportation facilities make their influence felt in such various ways as causing perishable food products to spoil, delaying the shipment of the huge quantities of building material which are required for new construction enterprises, holding back the shipment of grain to the ports where it is to be loaded for export, etc.

The Soviet railroad system has expanded to

some extent by comparison with prewar conditions. In 1913 Russia had 59,000 kilometers of railroad lines and the amount of freight carried during that year was 132,000,000 tons. In 1927–28, the year before the Five-Year Plan went into operation, the length of the railroad lines was 77,000 kilometers and the amount of freight carried was 151,000,000 tons. Since that time there has been an enormous increase in the burden of freight placed upon the railroads. The plan for 1931 calls for the shipment on the railroads of 330,000,000 tons of freight, which exceeds by almost 50,000,000 tons the maximum freight estimate of the Five-Year Plan for 1932–33.

The technical improvement of the Soviet railroads has not kept up with this vast increase of freight. In 1929–30, when the capital investments in industry increased by 130% over the preceding year, the amount of capital invested in transport increased by only 52%. Writing in the magazine *Boshevik* on "Transport on The Threshold of The Third Year of The Five-Year Plan," V. Dokukin gives the following characterization of the technical condition of the Soviet railroads:

During the last few years not one of the basic elements in transportation (roadbed, track, rolling stock, means of communication) has made any considerable steps forward in technical reconstruction. The length of the lines in use grew extremely slowly: from 1925–26 until 1929–30 the average growth of these lines increased by only one per cent. The car reserve consists 90% of antiquated, feeble, two-axle cars, tanks and platforms. The extraordinarily high percentage (74) of closed cars did not make it possible to mechanize the loading and unloading processes with such bulky forms of freight as coal, ore, building materials, etc. The sharp lack of open cars is already becoming an obstacle to the construction of big mines. The engines are also to a considerable degree antiquated.

A Soviet railroad commission, headed by Mr. Sulimov, Vice-Commissar for Transport, spent several months in America studying transportation methods in the early part of 1930; and in the summer of that year Ralph Budd, president of the Great Northern Railway Co., of the United States, at the invitation of the Soviet authorities, made an extensive tour of inspection which took him over all the principal Soviet railroads. His recommendations for improvement and reconstruction were summarized in a memorandum which Mr. Budd communicated to the author in Russia last summer, and which may be reproduced here as giving an outside expert's view of the condition of the Soviet railroads and the main needs in the field of reconstruction: [1]

[1] See an article by Mr. Budd, " The Soviet Railway System," *Economic Review of the Soviet Union*, V, 464.

I can point out some essential differences between the railways here and those in the United States. The most noticeable thing is that our freight cars are larger, averaging over 80,000 pounds and having an average length of 45 feet. We think the larger cars make the handling of bulk traffic easier because so many less units have to be handled. Moreover, all cars in the United States are equipped with automatic couplers and air brakes. Without these appliances the American railways could not handle the traffic they do with the relatively large proportion of single-track mileage that exists there. Of even more importance than increasing the capacity of the railways is the greater safety of operation which the abandonment of the old hand coupler and hand brake has brought us.

Applying automatic couplers would be the first step that I would take in improving the railways here. Simultaneously with this I would equip freight cars with air brakes as rapidly as practicable. It is not necessary to do this all at once. The railways of the United States applied air brakes over a period of several years. There would be great economy in adopting large cars in connection with this program of improvement, because less than half as many cars would be required and the cost of couplings and brakes would be correspondingly reduced.

Next to the small cars, which have hand-operated couplings and most of which have no brakes, the most obvious difference in freight trains here and in America is that the trains here are so much shorter. I do not know of any reason why small trains should continue to prevail here, any more than they did in America. Larger trains, of course, will require larger locomotives. We have found in the United States that handling a smaller number of the larger trains made up of larger cars and drawn by larger locomotives is more economical for a given amount of traffic than handling a larger number of small trains with small cars and locomotives.

The railway tracks of the Soviet Union ride comfortably at moderate speeds, but the rail, especially at the joints, is usually not well supported. More and larger ties are necessary for economy of both timber and rail, and the use of more and larger ties will at the same time reduce the amount of labor necessary to maintain the track. The ties now being used in the Soviet Union tracks are wearing out comparatively soon, and the life of the rail is also being greatly shortened because the ties are only about 70% as thick as they should be and because only about 75% as many ties are used as should be.

Another deficiency in most of the tracks over which we have traveled is the use of sand, instead of gravel, for ballast. There are places where gravel is used, and there the track is better than where it is surfaced with sand.

There are many differences between the methods of operation here and in the United States. The frequent slowing down and stopping of trains and the frequent delays of freight which occur in the Soviet Union are due in large part to the manner of dispatching trains.

In many respects the work which the railways here have to do is similar to that done by the railways of the United States. The commodities handled are in general the same; the long distances are also the same, although there are no distances in the United States comparable with those of Siberia. The topography of the country traversed by our railways is quite similar to that of the Soviet Union, except that the crossings of the Rocky and Cascade Mountains are more difficult and higher than any in the Soviet Union.

Perhaps the outstanding idea behind the improvements made in recent years to the American railways has been the willingness to adopt improved facilities, cars and locomotives as soon as they have proved satisfactory, even though it has been necessary in many instances to abandon old facilities and retire old equipment in order to get the advantages from the new. The railways of the Soviet Union are in a favorable position in this respect because they have had many years' use of their present equipment and facilities and they may now take advantage of the experience of other railways in their reconstruction program. The tracks of the railways of the Soviet Union have a gauge three and a half inches wider than those of the United States. This favorable feature will make easy the use of large cars and locomotives.

Mr. Budd's basic suggestions have been accepted and are included in the official Soviet plan for the reconstruction of the railroad system. The more important of these suggestions, such as the introduction of automatic couplers, air brakes, automatic signaling and larger locomotives, require a considerable expenditure of metal, of which there is a chronic shortage, and they will consequently be introduced rather gradually. Some of these changes will not be fully accomplished until after the completion of the Five-Year Plan.

Apart from these more far-reaching reconstruction schemes, immediate measures are being taken to insure greater efficiency on the railroads. Labor discipline is being tightened; special courts are set up to try persons charged with gross violations of the rules governing safety, and in a few cases death sentences have been imposed on individuals who were found guilty of causing disastrous wrecks through culpable negligence.

Capital investments in transport during 1931 are to be raised from 1,800,000,000 rubles in 1929-30 to 3,185,000,000 rubles; daily loadings of freight cars are to increase from 46,000 to 64,000, and the average daily run of a freight car is to increase from 90 to 135 kilometers. The president of the State Planning Commission, V. V. Kuibishev, addressing the Soviet Central Executive Committee on January 5, 1931, declared:

The present situation with transport is very strained. Everyone knows of the disorganization of passenger movement which everyone must feel directly. The situation is no better with the movement of freight. An enormous quantity of the ore which is so necessary for metallurgy is now lying unmoved; 2,000,000 tons of grain, which can not be transported at the present moment are lying unmoved, and this is also true of a vast amount of consumable goods. Such a condition is no longer tolerable. Therefore during 1931 we must invest vast resources in transport to push it ahead considerably, in order to re-equip it technically. We must give the transportation system in 1931 very strained tasks.

It remains to be seen whether transport will cope adequately with these "strained tasks."

The loading of freight cars was one of the fields in which the planned achievements in 1930 were most regularly left inadequately fulfilled.

Besides thoroughly renovating and reconstructing its existing railroad system the Soviet Union is building a number of new lines, among which the most important is probably a projected railway between Kuznetzk, in Siberia, center of a huge coal field which is in a comparatively early stage of development, and the site of a projected new steel plant, and Magnitogorsk, in the southern Urals, where the largest steel plant in Europe is now in process of construction. In transport, as in industry, there is a tendency to demand that building should be more concentrated, so that quicker immediate results can be derived from the new construction projects.

(g) Finance

The Soviet financial system is quite different from that of Western Europe and America. Its main differentiating characteristics are that Soviet currency is not convertible into gold, and is legally isolated to a large extent from contact with foreign currencies, both the importation and the exportation of Soviet rubles being forbidden. The Soviet State Bank and other credit institutions give rubles in exchange for foreign currency at a fixed rate of a little less than two rubles to the dollar; but the reverse operation of giving foreign currency in exchange for rubles is performed only in special cases and not at all as a general rule.

In short, the Soviet currency is designed as a medium only for internal exchange. It falls under three categories.[1] There are banknotes of the State Bank, so-called *chervontzi*, or notes issued in 10-ruble and larger denominations. Against these, according to the law, there must be a reserve of 25% in gold, precious metals and foreign currency. There are also Treasury notes, issued in 1-, 3- and 5-ruble denominations, which have no special backing. At first the issue of Treasury notes was limited to 50% of the value of the *chervontzi* in circulation. Recently, however, this limit was raised to 100%. A certain amount of poor quality silver, copper and bronze coins is utilized as small change.

In the matter of currency issue the Five-Year Plan was exceeded in rather undesirable fashion in 1930. The Five-Year Plan contemplated a maximum currency issue of 3,200,000,000 rubles

[1] For a historical account of the currency see James R. Mood, *Handbook of Foreign Currency and Exchange*, p. 152–156 (Department of Commerce, Trade Promotion Series No. 102).

in 1932–33, the annual increase in currency issue being proportioned more or less carefully to the estimated growth of goods and commercial turnover. Under the pressure of the need for currency, both for financing the growth of industry and for buying up the peasants' produce, and under the influence of the fact that labor productivity did not increase, and costs of production during 1930 did not decrease as much as had been planned, the issue of currency exceeded all the projected limits. The amount of money in circulation grew from 1,970,800,000 rubles on October 1, 1928, to 2,642,200,000 rubles on the same date in 1929, and to 4,263,900,000 rubles on October 1, 1930.[1]

By the time this last figure had been reached (the issue of currency increased especially rapidly during the summer months of 1930), the country was faced with a problem of inflation. This tendency, to be sure, did not find the customary means of expression in a swift upturn of prices, necessitating corresponding increases of wages and salaries, which, in turn, demand the printing of more paper money. Prices in the Soviet Union more than in any other country are under state control because practically all industries and the lion's share of retail trade are in the hands

[1] These figures were supplied to the author by the State Planning Commission.

of the state. Consequently there was no great variation in the prices of staple commodities, and wages and salaries, according to plan, were pushed up at an average rate of about 6% a year.

But the excessive emission of currency made itself felt unfavorably in several ways. It unquestionably intensified the goods shortage by creating vastly more nominal purchasing power than could be satisfied. It was reflected in the sweeping rise of prices on the private market, the superfluity of money and the scarcity of goods combining to drive prices to extreme heights wherever the law of supply and demand was permitted to work unchecked. It generated in the population, especially in the peasants, a contempt and distrust for money, which led to much open or surreptitious bartering of town for country products. During the summer months an acute shortage of small change developed, because these coins, which were believed to have more value than the paper money, were being systematically hoarded.

A sharp turn in Soviet monetary policy became visible in the autumn of 1930. While Soviet economists deny the theoretical possibility of inflation under socialist economic conditions, nevertheless when industrial and agricultural prices are kept stable through centralized regulation in the " socialist sector " of economic life, and only the much smaller " private sector " experiences fluctuations in the price level as a result of the increased issue of currency, the practical inconveniences of the free use of the printing press during 1930 were visible and disturbing. Consequently, in the autumn of 1930 a " no emission " financial policy was inaugurated; and the state budget and " unified financial plan "[1] for 1931, adopted by the Soviet Central Executive Committee in January, 1931, were based on the same principle.

The " unified financial plan," it may be noted, is a sort of enlarged budget which includes, besides ordinary budget receipts and expenditures, a much wider range of receipts and expenditures connected with the economic development of the country. Its scope was defined by Gregory F. Grinko, Commissar for Finance, when in his speech before the Soviet Central Executive Committee on January 5, 1931, he said:

We lay before you not only a state budget, but a unified financial plan, embracing the state budget, all the resources of the credit organizations of our country, and all the means of the economic organizations of the socialized sector, not

[1] The text of the unified financial plan is given in appendix XIII, p. 234–243.

only of state industry, transport and cooperation, but of such a young member of our socialized economic system as are the collective farms.

The revenue under the unified financial plan for 1930 was estimated at 23,427,000,000 rubles, while for 1931 the plan called for receipts of 31,755,300,000 rubles, the proposed expenditures for 1931 being calculated at 1,500,000,000 rubles less than the receipts. In this way it is estimated that a reserve of a billion and a half rubles will be created, so that any possible deficit in any branch of economic life can be covered without resorting to the printing press. The unified financial plan for 1930 included on its income side about a billion and a half rubles of fresh currency issue, whereas the plan for 1931 definitely excludes this resource. It is estimated that almost two thirds of the national income of 49,000,000,000 rubles will be redistributed under the unified financial plan.

The increased resources which are projected for 1931 are based on the expectation of greater income from state enterprises, as a result of the combined influence of increased output, lowered costs of production and heightened labor productivity, larger yield from taxes, which, again, are mostly paid by state and cooperative industrial and commercial organizations, greater " attraction of the resources of the population " through investments in loans and deposits in savings banks, etc. There are few private traders left to tax in the towns; but the agricultural tax, a general income tax levied on the peasants, will be increased from 415,000,000 rubles in 1928-29 to 500,000,000 rubles in 1931, and a special levy of 200,000,000 rubles will be made on the individual peasants, a fact which will quite possibly kill two birds with one stone, from the Soviet standpoint, by extracting the surplus funds which the peasants accumulated by charging high prices for their produce on the free market, and by causing many individual peasants to see the advantages of collective farming. In general, it seems probable that during 1931 a strong effort will be made to restore a more even balance between the currency in circulation and the amount of goods which may be bought by diminishing the supply of the former and increasing that of the latter.

The Soviet state debt, which was 1,300,700,000 rubles on October 1, 1928, increased to 2,541,-000,000 rubles on the same date in 1929, and to 3,432,200,000 rubles in October, 1930.[1] It is expected that state loans will realize another 1,300,000,000 rubles during 1931. Such calcu-

[1] Figures supplied by the State Planning Commission.

lations can be made with a fair degree of certainty, because subscriptions to state loans in the Soviet Union are socially, if not legally, almost compulsory for workers and employees in the state service. Attempts to distribute these loans among the peasants have hitherto been less successful, but will probably be intensified during the coming year.

Despite the efforts which are made to persuade the population to deposit money in savings banks the accumulations of these institutions in the Soviet Union are not very impressive. Savings bank deposits increased from 172,300,000 rubles on October 1, 1927, to 707,500,000 rubles on December 1, 1930, the deposits therefore amounting to less than five rubles per capita. Two factors help to discourage saving in Russia. In the first place, many forms of misfortune, such as illness and disability incurred during work, are provided for under a system of compulsory state insurance, which applies to all wage-workers. The second factor is uncertainty as to the future value of money and of its buying power in years to come. The desire of the average Soviet citizen to spend rather than to hoard his money contributes to accentuate the goods shortage.

An important financial innovation was the

decree of January 30, 1930, which established the so-called credit reform. This reform substituted banking credit for goods credit and aimed at diminishing the need for the use of money by prescribing for state economic organizations a scheme of payment between themselves based on checks and credit transfers. The State Bank became a sort of central clearing house for these payments. The credit reform, according to the book, *Credit Reform*, by A. A. Blum and B. M. Berlatzky (State Financial Publishing House, 1930), pursued the following objectives:

(1) The bringing of full clarity into the mutual relations between the banks and the economic organizations.

(2) Strengthening of the planned element in the activity of the banks.

(3) Tightening, with the help of the bank apparatus, of the planned discipline of the economic organizations.

(4) Establishment of direct connection between the crediting of an economic organization and its fulfilment of the economic tasks which have been imposed upon it.

(5) Extension and deepening of individual accounting responsibility in the enterprises.

(6) Bringing the credit organizations closer to the lower branches of the economic organizations.

(7) Concentration of all accounts of the economic organizations between themselves in the banks.

(8) Strengthening of the rôle of the State Bank as the central and, in the future, the sole institution of short-term credit and organ of socialist accounting.

(9) Regulation and strengthening of the system of agricultural credit, with simultaneous strengthening of the productive-economic regulation of the collective farms by the proletarian state.

(10) Development of settling accounts without cash.

There were some difficulties in putting this credit reform into practice and the increased issue of currency during 1930 indicated that the new system did not relieve the need for money as much as had been expected and also that " the tightening of the planned discipline of the economic organizations," in some cases at least, was an ideal rather than a reality. However, the Soviet financial system seems certain to develop along the lines marked out by the credit reform. Large scale settlements without cash become increasingly practicable as more and more of the country's economic life is placed under centralized socialist control.

The effort to carry through the unified financial plan for 1931 without resorting to currency issue will furnish an interesting test of the Soviet claim that inflation has not been an element in the swift industrialization of the country without aid from foreign capital. It will be an added means of judging the ability of the various state industrial, agricultural and transport enterprises to realize the tasks which have been assigned them in the field of reducing production costs.

In general, the Soviet financial system affords an interesting example of a " managed " currency which, like all the other resources of the country, is placed entirely at the service of the socialist reorganization of the country. The organization of the budget, of taxation and of credit has been avowedly a weapon of class warfare, an instrument for pumping resources out of the private into the socialized sector of national economic life. This has been especially true during the last two or three years. Many a ruined *kulak* and Nepman, or private trader, could testify to the accuracy of I. Miroshnikov's observation in *Izvestia* of November 13, 1930:

> In the sharp class struggle of the past year the Soviet finances represented a powerful weapon of proletarian offensive. The financial system gave everything that the growth and socialist reconstruction of the economic life of the country demanded of it and emerged ready for new battles.

It is interesting to speculate on what will be the future of money in the completely socialized economic order toward which the Communist Party is now driving. What will be the situation when the last peasant has joined a collective farm and the hardiest trader has been obliged to stop what the Communists regard as his nefarious and anti-social activity? For the immediate future money as a medium of exchange seems safe, so far as the efforts of the Soviet economic authorities can make it so. In fact, the Communists hope to lend greater real purchasing power to the ruble in so far as they are able to increase the amount of foodstuffs and manufactured goods available for sale in state and cooperative stores.

For the more remote future the problem of money remains more or less open. Theoretically, when all the peasants are organized in collective farms as completely as the city workers are organized in factories, a vast amount of moneyless

103

exchange could take place. On the other hand, it may be that, even in an economic order which is more thoroughly socialized than the present one in the Soviet Union, it will be found that money wages are preferable to any kind of rationing system because they will give the individual greater latitude in satisfying his special needs and wants.

CHAPTER III

THE REMOLDING OF RUSSIAN AGRICULTURE

W E must not for too long a period of time base the Soviet power and the socialist structure on two different foundations, on the foundation of the largest and most unified socialist industry and on the foundation of the most divided and backward small peasant farming. It is necessary gradually, but systematically and stubbornly, to remake agriculture on a new technical basis, on the basis of big production, pulling it up to the socialist industry. Either we solve this problem, and then final victory is guaranteed, or we retreat from it without solving it, and then the return to capitalism may become an unavoidable development.

This excerpt from a speech delivered by Stalin before the Central Committee of the Communist Party in November, 1928, is an appropriate commentary on the whole trend of Soviet agrarian policy during the last three years. In the drive toward the goal of a unified economic system, responsive to centralized planning, agriculture was the last and hardest nut to be cracked.

105

It must never be forgotten that the Revolution of 1917, while socialist in the towns, was individualist or, as the Communists might say, "petty bourgeois" in the villages. Factories, banks, railroads, communal enterprises were transferred to state or communal ownership. But the land was simply redistributed among individual possessors, the country squires being expropriated and the *kulaks*, or richer peasants, having their allotments reduced in favor of the poor and middle class peasants.

Lenin as a theoretician told a doubting audience of peasants gathered in the Congress of Peasants' Deputies in the spring of 1917 that their economic salvation lay in large scale farms, organized by the state and provided with modern machinery and equipment. But Lenin the statesman knew the mood of the peasant masses so well that he did not attempt to carry out his theoretical agrarian program after the Bolshevik seizure of power in November, 1917. The Bolshevik Land Law aimed to satisfy the hunger of the peasants for land by decreeing the expropriation of the larger estates without attempting to deny the small peasant owner the right to farm his land on an individual basis.

During the period of civil war and military

communism there were experiments in state and cooperative farming; but these experiments as a rule were not very successful. The property-owning instinct of the peasants was strong and the Government was in no position to supply the tractors and other modern machines on which large scale farming depends for effectiveness.

From 1921, when the New Economic Policy was proclaimed, until 1928, when a sharp new turn began to manifest itself in Soviet agrarian policy, more than 95% of the land was in the hands of individual users. The Russian peasant, to be sure, did not enjoy all the customary rights of private ownership. Legally all land was state property and could not be bought or sold. Each village community allotted the land in its possession among its households, the share of each household being determined by the number of members. If, for instance, the share of each member amounted to three acres, a household with ten members would be entitled to 30 acres of land, a family of five to 15, and so on.

Despite the prohibition of the purchase and sale of land, and despite the fact that Soviet social and economic measures were framed with a view to checking the increase of the *kulaks* and helping the poorer peasants, a considerable measure of inequality developed among the peasants during the first years of the New Economic Policy. Although the Revolution and civil war cast all old property rights into the melting pot, the peasants did not all start out under the Nep on a basis of equality. Some had saved more cattle and machinery than others. As soon as the incentive of free trade was restored, inequalities of shrewdness, thrift, farming ability, etc., manifested themselves. Communist economists divided the peasants into the three more or less loosely defined classes of *kulaks*, *seredniaks*, or middle class peasants, and *biedniaks*, or poor; and the avowed Communist policy, especially in recent years, has been to combat the *kulaks*, while maintaining a political union with the middle class peasants and basing their power firmly only on the poor.

At first the recovery of agriculture went more rapidly and smoothly than the recovery of industry. The population of the cities had greatly diminished during the civil war; and the problem of adequately provisioning the towns was quickly solved on the basis of the increased agricultural output which came as a natural result of the stoppage of requisitions, the restoration of freedom of internal trade, the end of civil war and the re-establishment of order throughout the country.

In 1923–24, only a year after the end of the great famine in the Valley of the Volga, Russia exported about 3,000,000 tons of grain, which was between 25 and 30% of the average prewar annual grain export. A drought in 1924 stopped the export of grain; but it was resumed in 1925–26 and 1926–27.

In the winter of 1927–28, however, the Soviet Union found itself faced with a crisis of agrarian supply, especially in the field of grain output, which was destined to have far-reaching consequences on the development of Soviet agrarian policy. This crisis was a result of several causes. The cities were filling up rapidly as the industries revived; the purchasing power of the wage-earning classes was increasing, and there was a consequent steady growth in the demand for foodstuffs for the non-agricultural population and also for industrial raw material.

There was, however, no corresponding progress in agriculture. Individual peasant output, under the restrictions of the Soviet agrarian legislation, had almost reached its limit of development. The development of a prosperous class of farmers, capable of raising a substantial marketable surplus, was obstructed by the political and economic measures directed against the *kulaks*. The poor peasants scarcely produced enough to feed themselves. The middle class peasant household, with its one, or at the most two horses, and its 20 or 30 acres of land scattered about in inconvenient and uneconomic little strips, in accordance with the traditional Russian village rules of land distribution, also yielded little surplus. The big producers of exportable grain in prewar times — the private landlord estates — had been annihilated by the Revolution; and there was nothing to take their place.

Moreover, even if the 26,000,000 small holdings which existed in the Soviet Union had been mechanically capable of producing a large quantity of marketable crops, they had no very strong incentive to do so. Ever since 1925 a sharp shortage of manufactured goods had manifested itself. The Soviet factories could not produce textiles, boots and other articles of everyday consumption fast enough to meet the need, and very little could be imported from abroad, because of the slow growth of foreign trade and the fact that machinery and essential raw materials constituted the lion's share of Soviet imports. The peasant had no adequate spending outlet for his money. State loans and savings banks did not attract him. He could not, as he would perhaps have done in former times, invest his surplus savings in land.

Perhaps the final determining factor in bringing about the difficulties with grain supply in 1927–28 was the talk about the menace of war, in which Soviet leaders freely indulged after the breach of relations with Great Britain in the spring of 1927. To the peasant mind the threat of war suggested the advisability of hoarding grain and any other food which was available.

Instead, therefore, of being able to proceed with the usual exportation of grain, the Soviet authorities found themselves confronted with an actual shortage of supply for internal needs. Vigorous so-called " extraordinary measures " were applied; the local officials put sufficient pressure on the peasants to extract their surplus grain. In some cases persons accused of " speculation," or of hoarding grain, were arrested and banished; in others, mere hints of arrest were sufficient to accomplish the purpose. These " extraordinary measures " represented the first blow at the Nep, under which the peasant had been supposedly free to dispose of his produce as he saw fit.

The Soviet Government in 1928 was faced with an agrarian dilemma. Merely to resort to the old methods of requisitioning, under more or less thinly disguised forms, promised nothing but further discouragement of the peasant's individual enterprise. Some sort of radical break with the whole existing system of agricultural production was necessary, if the economic development of the country was not to be arrested by a chronic shortage of grain and agricultural raw material.

Broadly speaking, there were two alternatives which offered an escape from the dilemma of agrarian underproduction and stagnation. The productivity of agriculture could have been increased by letting down the artificial barriers which stood in the way of the peasant's development into a rich farmer, by restoring private property in land, by helping the more prosperous peasants to extend their planted acreage and output instead of blocking them at every point with heavy discriminatory taxation and other methods. This line of policy would have corresponded with the individualist psychology of the peasants and was favored by many non-Communist Russian agrarian specialists.

But, from the Communist standpoint, such a policy would have been inconsistent with what was regarded as the proper development of the Revolution. By giving a free hand to the *kulak* it would have enthroned private capitalism in

112

Russia's basic industry, which is agriculture; it would have postponed for a long time, if not forever, the ideal of introducing socialist principles in farming; it would have smashed the prospect of a planned economic order. Experience had shown that, however successfully the state planning organs might lay down plans of development for industry or wholesale trade or other branches which were under centralized state control, it was impossible to include adequately in the sphere of planning the millions of peasant households, each of which was pursuing its own direct gain, with little regard for the interests of the impersonal state.

So the Party chose a policy which involved many more political and economic risks and hardships in the first years of its application, but which, if successful, meant victory and not defeat for socialism, and the elimination of the last major class that stood outside the framework of the socialist order — the individualist peasantry. The main elements in this policy were: productive cooperation of the poor and middle class peasants in so-called *kolkhozi*, or collective farms; economic extermination of the *kulaks;* and intensive development of *sovkhozi*, or state farms. This policy did not go into effect at a uniform rate of speed all at once. The leaders of the so-called "right deviation" in the Communist Party — Rykov, Tomsky and Bukharin — were strongly opposed to certain features of this program of drastic rural socialization; and their influence in 1928 was strong enough to cause certain delays and waverings.

In 1929, however, the rigorous policy of socialization at maximum speed went ahead faster and faster. The requisitioning of grain at fixed prices in the autumn of 1929 was more sweeping and ruthless than at any time since the civil war. The inflow of peasants into the newly organized collective farms assumed tremendous proportions. Part of it was due to the many preferences which were now being given to collective farms: allotment of the choicest land, lower taxes, first consideration in the supply of credits, machinery, manufactured goods, etc. Part of it was also due to the fact that, under the system of heavy taxes and grain requisitions the life of the comparatively prosperous individual peasant was being made quite impossible.

In the latter part of December, 1929, Stalin in a public speech indorsed a practice that was already being carried out in many rural districts where collectivization was widespread, namely, the expropriation of the *kulaks* and their " liquidation as a class." Under this practice the houses, livestock and machinery of the *kulaks* were confiscated, and they were either exiled to remote parts of the country or driven out of the village and left to shift for themselves on unused land, with such scanty supplies of cattle and machinery as might be left to them. This method was obviously a strong compelling factor in bringing the middle class peasants to see the advantages of collectivization. According to a speech delivered before the Sixteenth Congress of the Communist Party by the Commissar for Agriculture, Y. A. Yakovlev, about 20% of the resources of the collective farms came from confiscated *kulak* property which was turned over to them.

Beginning with the autumn of 1929, under the influence of all these factors, the collective farm movement grew by leaps and bounds. The Five-Year Plan had originally contemplated the collectivization of from 15 to 20% of the peasant households by 1933; but this figure was soon exceeded. An original plan for the collectivization of 10% of the peasant households in 1931 was soon replaced by a new plan calling for the collectivization of 30%. At the end of February, when the numerical highwater mark of the collective farm movement was reached, the percentage of collectivization was estimated at 55 or 57.

But just at this time a severe crisis made itself felt; and the Party leadership, without abandoning the basic idea of collective farming, found it expedient to introduce drastic modifications in the methods which were being employed to promote this end. During January and February the use of sheer and undisguised compulsion to drive the peasants into the collective farms steadily increased. The measure of expropriation which was supposed to be applied only against the 4 or 5% of peasant households which were regarded as *kulak* were applied to many middle class peasant families. Peasants who refused to join collective farms were in some cases arrested or threatened with arrest and exile.

There were many attempts to turn the newly organized collective farms into pure communes, where all property would be shared equally. This idea commended itself to the poor peasants on whom the Communist local authorities leaned more and more heavily as they carried out a sharper and sharper policy of destruction of the richer elements in the village; but it strongly alienated the middle class peasants, who constitute the numerical majority in the Russian countryside and whose cooperation was necessary if collectivization was to have a fair prospect of success.

All these excesses provoked sporadic outbursts of peasant resentment, especially in regions where the movement for collective farming was especially weak, as in the provinces around Moscow and Leningrad, which do not raise a grain surplus, and in some of the non-Russian regions, inhabited by minor nationalities, in the Caucasus and Central Asia. Much more serious than these outbursts, which were quickly suppressed, was the wholesale slaughtering of cattle which took place all over the Soviet Union. This was partly due to the influence of the doomed *kulaks*, who, having nothing to lose, killed their own cattle as rapidly as possible and urged their neighbors to do likewise. In Lower Volga regions which the writer visited last summer, it was generally said that the ruthless grain requisitions of the preceding autumn had also helped to cause the destruction of livestock, because the peasants needed the meat for food after being deprived of their grain and also, as a result of the requisitions, lacked fodder for their animals.

Moreover, the sweeping numerical growth of the collective farms had far outstripped the possibilities of providing them with trained leaders and agricultural experts and with tractors and other large machines. In the light of all these considerations, a modification of policy was clearly necessary if the country was to be spared the risk of a first rate agricultural politico-economic crisis.

A recognition of this fact was first heralded by Stalin's article, " Giddiness From Success," published in the Soviet press on March 2, 1930. In this article he severely rebuked local officials and Party workers who were attempting to establish collective farms through the agency of administrative pressure. He censured the tendency of regional authorities to compete with each other in swelling the figures of collectivization, regardless of the preparedness of the region for this step.

" In a number of regions of Turkestan," Stalin wrote, " efforts were made to overtake the leading regions of the Soviet Union by threatening with military force and the deprivation of irrigation water those peasants who did not wish to enter collective farms. Such methods can lead only to the strengthening of our enemies and the discrediting of the idea of collective farming. To irritate a member of a collective farm by socializing his living quarters, his small cattle and his chickens when cooperative farming is not yet firmly established, is it not clear that such a policy can benefit only our sworn enemies?"

Stalin's letter was followed by a series of Party resolutions and government decrees,[1] calculated to eliminate the abuses which were threatening the program of collectivization with failure. The principle was definitely laid down that the basic type of collective farm should be not the commune but the *artel*, or agricultural productive cooperative. A distinct line of demarcation was drawn between what should and what should not be socialized in the *artel*. So, while peasants joining this type of organization were obliged to surrender title to their land, working cattle and large machinery, which passed into communal ownership, they were assured personal possession of their homes, gardens, chickens, sheep and pigs, and were also allowed to keep one cow for personal use. Orders were given to the effect that those peasants who had been " collectivized " against their will should be allowed to take back their property and return to individual farming, if they so desired. While the policy of expropriating the *kulaks* remained in force, restitution was to be made to those middle class and poor peasants who had been expropriated by the arbitrary decision of local authorities.

Simultaneously with the renunciation of crude administrative force as a means of creating collec-

[1] The more important of these are reproduced textually in the appendices.

tive farms, there was an effort to make the latter more attractive by granting the members certain supplementary benefits, in the way of tax reductions and exemption, release from earlier debts to state organizations, etc. The right of the peasant, regardless of whether he was or was not a member of a collective farm, to sell his produce freely on the market was reaffirmed. This right, it should be noted, applied primarily to garden products, eggs, butter, milk, etc. Both collective farms and individual peasants, the former openly, the latter by various forms of " social " pressure, are required to sell their surplus grain to the state and cooperative organs at fixed prices.

As a result of the relaxation of administrative pressure there was a substantial exodus of peasants from the newly organized collective farms. The proportion of collectivized households dropped from 55 or 57% at the end of February to somewhere between 20 and 25% in the summer. Here it remained more or less stable for a time, but in the autumn a new inflow of peasants into the collective farms was noted.[1] The withdrawal of

[1] This inflow continued at a rapid pace throughout the winter; and by April 10, 1931, 45.2% of the peasant households had entered the collective farms. This indicates that the Communist Party program of drawing at least 50% of the peasant homesteads into collective farms by the end of 1931 will be fulfilled. The percentage of collectivization on April 10 was highest in the North Caucasus (80.6), in the Volga German Republic (85.5) in the Crimea (81) and in the steppe region of Ukraina (79.4). It had exceeded 26% in the Moscow and Leningrad regions.

the peasants was not evenly distributed over the whole country. In Central and Northern Russia it assumed an overwhelming character. In Moscow Oblast, a territory with a population of some 10,000,000, the percentage of collectivization fell from 70 to 7.

But in districts which were more important from the productive standpoint, in the rich grain belt of Southern Ukraina, the North Caucasus and the Lower Volga, 40 or 50% of the peasants stayed in the new collective farms. Here the new form of organization had struck deeper roots; more efforts were made to persuade the peasants to remain, and the use of the tractor, which is a cementing force in holding a collective farm together, was most developed in these rich steppe grain regions.

The spring planting campaign and the following harvest represented the first big decisive test of the Soviet experiment in mass collectivization of agriculture. On the whole, this test was met successfully. Notwithstanding the elimination of the *kulaks*, who had formerly been the most productive individual farmers, notwithstanding the mood of confusion and discouragement which was generated among the individual peasants by the excesses of forced collectivization, the planted area increased by almost 10,000,000 hectares.[1] This was due to the sweeping growth registered by the collective farms, which increased their planted area by 50%, ploughing up an additional 30,000,000 acres.

Favorable weather conditions lent added effectiveness to the increased planted area. The yield of grain is estimated to have increased by 15,000,000 tons; the cotton crop increased by 60% and the sugar beet crop by 150%. Inasmuch as these gains were obtained in the "socialized sector" of agriculture, it is natural that Communist policy should foresee the future development of agriculture primarily through the extension of this sector. It is now planned that half the peasant households shall be collectivized by the end of 1931; and it is reported that during the months of September and October, 1930, half a million peasant families entered collective farms.

The collective farms, which, given a continuation of the present policy, seem destined to become the predominant form in Russian agriculture during the next two or three years, may be divided into three categories, as regards organization. These are the commune, the *artel*, and the cooperative

[1] According to the statement of the President of the State Planning Commission, V. V. Kuibishev, in *Izvestia* for December 4, 1930.

for common tilling of the land. In the commune all property, with the exception of a few simple articles of personal use, is socialized, and the members take their meals in common. In the *artel*, which is now regarded as the most suitable form of organization, in the majority of cases the peasant, as has been described, retains his home, garden, small animals, etc., while surrendering his land, machinery and working animals to common ownership, and working with his fellows in the organization under the direction of an elected management. The cooperative for common tilling of the land is a simpler form of organization, recommended for regions where, for some reason, the peasants are unprepared for complete collectivism. In such cooperatives the members pool their land, machinery and working cattle at sowing and harvest times without, however, renouncing title to possession, as they must do in the *artels*. Of the collectivized peasant households 73.5% belong to artels, 18% to cooperatives for common tilling of the land, and 8.5% to communes.[1]

Management of the collective farm is vested in a board, elected at a meeting of the members. Field work is under the direction of farm foremen,

---

[1] According to a statement made to the writer by a representative of the Collective Farm Center in the summer of 1930.

or "brigadiers," who may be appointed by the management or elected by the groups of workers in the fields. Although the collective farm is supposed to be a voluntary cooperative organization, various means are adopted to insure a considerable measure of state control over its activities. Last winter and spring 25,000 picked industrial workers, mostly Communists, were sent into the villages to promote collectivization. Some of these were appointed managers of collective farms, others obtained posts in the local Soviet and cooperative systems; but the whole mass of the "twenty-five thousand," as they were called, exercised a watchful guardianship over the state interests, as opposed to the immediate private property instincts of the peasant, in such matters as labor discipline, sale of surplus produce to state and cooperative organizations, and not on the private market, etc.

Moreover, the collective farms are included in a nation-wide organized system, which, after passing through several stages, reaches its top in the Collective Farm Center in Moscow. Semi-mandatory instructions, production plans and credits, which may be granted or withheld, depending upon the carrying out of the instructions and the fulfillment of the plans, filter down from the Collective Farm Center through several regional links to the individual collective farm. After a variety of experiments the following scheme of distributing income in the collective farms has been generally adopted. After the harvest is realized deductions are made to meet the following needs and expenses: seeds and fodder; taxes and insurance; contributions to the " untouchable fund " which is maintained for the purchase of new machinery, for building, etc.; provision for debt payment; contributions, not to exceed 5%, for educational purposes and for the maintenance of the infirm; administrative expenses, which are not supposed to exceed 2 or 3% of the total available sum.

What is left after these first charges, is divided among the members according to the amount and quality of work which they have performed. An allotment of 5% of the total income is also reserved for distribution among members in accordance with the amount of property which they brought into the collective farm. This rather capitalistic feature was introduced after the wholesale slaughtering of cattle by the peasants showed the desirability of offering an inducement for the preservation of the former.

The increase of 50% in the planted area of the

collective farms is all the more striking if one considers that in recent years the general increase of the planted area in Russia has been very slight, never exceeding 5% in a single year. One explanation of this sweeping rise is greatly improved farm equipment. After the state farms, the collective farms receive first preference with tractors. If one takes into account that a considerable number of the poor peasant households included in the collective farms did not even possess horses when they existed on an individual basis, the increased possibilities of planting and sowing opened up by even an inadequate supply of tractors are obvious.

Under the Soviet agricultural system, moreover, the maximum continuous use is extracted from a tractor. If a state or collective farm has finished ploughing, planting or harvesting on its own land, it is supposed to throw its tractors and other larger machines over to the aid of some neighboring farm which is less well equipped. The differing agricultural seasons which prevail in varying parts of the Soviet Union make it possible to transfer tractors from the northern regions of Central Russia and Siberia to the more southern zones of Ukraina and the North Caucasus, or *vice versa*, as circumstances may dictate. That this continuous use is hard on the tractors and combines with other factors to cause an unduly high percentage of breakage, is another side of the picture. But the system has undoubtedly helped to solve one of the most pressing Soviet economic problems: the rapid pushing up of the acreage under cultivation.

An interesting development of modern Soviet agriculture, and one that seems destined to play an increasingly important rôle in the future, is the machine-tractor station. Attached to the machine-tractor station, which is equipped with a workshop, spare parts, facilities for repairs, etc., are a number of tractors. These are leased either to existing collective farms or to peasant households which agree to become collectivized in consideration of the aid which they receive from the station. The tractors do the ploughing, planting and harvesting, taking a fourth or a third of the crop in payment. Last year there were 157 tractor stations, and next year there will be over 1,000. It is estimated that next year these stations will attend to the working of almost 50,000,000 acres of collective farm land.

Advocates of Russia's new agricultural methods point to other advantages which are inherent in their adoption. Formerly the Russian countryside represented a curious patchwork of little plots of land, because the small peasant holdings were not, as a rule, concentrated in one place, but were scattered about in tiny strips of land, separated by ditches. Not only did this arrangement make the use of large machinery uneconomic, but the ditches were fertile breeders of insect parasites. In the collective farm, with its thousands of acres, the ditches are annihilated and there is free scope for the use of the tractor and the combine. Even in those collective farms which have not yet been equipped with tractors it is possible, under reasonably competent management, to utilize the combined resources of labor, working animals and machinery more rationally than if there were an irregular division of these resources among small individual holders. When a hundred or a thousand peasant families are working under a common discipline in a collective farm, they may carry out mutually beneficial building or irrigation projects on which no amount of persuasion could have induced them to combine when each family had its own homestead.

On the other hand, critics of the new agricultural methods, both among the peasants and among outside observers, would be inclined to argue that the loss of the sense of individual ownership robs the peasant of one of his strongest stimuli to hard work and careful handling of his tools and working animals. Certainly as yet the organization and productivity of labor in the collective farms leave much to be desired, and the question of how far the undeniably increased output, reflected by the resumption on a fairly large scale of grain exports in 1930–31, may be offset by breakage and wear-and-tear of valuable machinery, is a thorny economic problem which may not be settled for some years. However, the Communists are inclined to emphasize the incontestable achievement of increased production rather than to worry over dubious problems of cost accounting. All the plans for the future envisage a further rapid replacement of individual by state and collective farming.

Side by side with the new collective farms (*kolkhozi*) are developing state farms (*sovkhozi*), although the latter occupy a much smaller acreage. The difference between these two forms of socialized farming is that, whereas the collective farms are based on the contributed resources of their peasant members, the state farms are financed by the Government. The new big state farms, which have been established during the last two or three years under the direction of the Zernotrest, or State Grain Trust, are the largest agricultural enterprises in the world. The average size of the 210 state farms which the Zernotrest expects to be operating next spring is 200,000 acres. The organization of huge state farms was decided on as a means of overcoming the grain crisis of 1928; but the tempo of their development was much faster than was anticipated. The original plan called for the raising of 1,667,000 tons of grain in the last year of the *pyatiletka*, 1932–33; but as a matter of fact 1,024,700 tons were produced in 1930, while the projected figure for 1931 is 4,439,000 tons. This, in turn, will be doubled in 1932, according to present plans.

Most of the state farms have been established on unused land in Southeastern Russia, Siberia and Kazakstan. In organization they differ from the collective farms, being state and not cooperative enterprises. The managers are appointed by the Grain Trust, which is, of course, a state organization, and such permanent or temporary laborers as are needed are hired on a wage basis.

The state farms constitute an interesting experiment in the application of the most mechanized methods of modern agriculture to huge stretches of fresh land. Ten thousand tractors operated in the state farms last year. In 1931 23,000 new tractors are expected to facilitate the execution of the ambitious problem of more than quadrupling both the acreage and the yield on these huge farms, of which the largest, the " Giant " in the North Caucasus, ploughed up an area of almost 300,000 acres last year.

As the collective farm, as a general rule, yields more marketable grain or other produce than could be obtained from hundreds or thousands of small holdings occupying the same amount of land, so the state farm usually turns out a higher surplus than the collective farm. This is partly because the Soviet Government has taken special pains to equip the state farms with tractors, combines and other large machines, and partly because the state farm is organized on a different basis from the collective farm. No matter how much the latter may be under open or veiled state control, the wishes of the members in such matters as allotment of produce for their personal consumption can not safely be altogether ignored. A considerable amount of fodder must also be reserved for horses and other domestic animals. In the state farm, on the other hand, the employees are paid wages and have no right to a theoretical cooperative share of the produce. Operating on a fully mechanized basis, the state farm has only to provide food for its workers and seed for future use. The rest of its output is clear surplus gain for the state. The fact that it is highly mechanized makes it possible to operate with a much smaller number of workers.

The way of the state farm is not always smooth and easy. In connection with next year's planting program one already hears complaints to the effect that the supply of fuel and lubricating oil is not of adequate quality, that orders for machinery have not been filled with sufficient promptness, and so on. The Grain Trust in 1931 will obtain all its smaller agricultural implements from Soviet factories, and the quality of this production remains to be tested in some cases.

Apart from their purely agricultural productive functions, the state farms are supposed to serve as centers and bases for the collectivization of the surrounding countryside. One often finds a solid belt of collective farms around the area of a state farm. This is because the tractors of the state farm are leased to peasant villages, on condition that the latter adopt collective forms of farming. It is also alleged that peasants adopt cooperative methods of farming more readily when they see the possibilities of large output which are inherent in large scale mechanized farming.

In the beginning, state farms concentrated their

efforts almost exclusively upon grain. Now a number of large state cattle ranches and dairy and poultry farms have been established, and more are planned for the future.

This brings one to the weak spot in Russian agriculture at the present time — animal husbandry. The resistance of the more individually minded peasants was not strong enough to thwart the Soviet program of increased output of grain and other crops. But, finding expression in the wholesale destruction of livestock in the winter of 1929–30, it inflicted a deep, gaping wound on the country's reserves of domestic animals. This, in turn, has produced the crisis of supply, already noted, in meat, fats, dairy products, etc. Such kinds of raw material as are derived from animals — i. e., hides, wool and bristles — have also suffered. There have been varied estimates of the loss incurred in domestic animals; the following tabulated figures submitted by Gregory F. Grinko in *Pravda* of August 31, 1930, are perhaps as accurate as any others:

	1929	1930	1931
Large-horned cattle	67,230,600	51,823,100	58,871,000
In state farms......	204,700	493,100	3,545,000
In collective farms	384,100	3,510,000	8,480,000
In individual possession	66,614,800	47,820,000	46,846,000

	1929	1930	1931
Pigs	20,532,800	11,710,200	20,223,200
In state farms	54,400	200,400	818,100
In collective farms	126,600	380,000	3,340,000
In individual possession	20,345,500	11,129,800	16,065,100
Sheep	132,758,700	89,287,000	102,680,000
In state farms	1,200,000	3,642,400	4,828,200
In collective farms	678,200	2,528,000	6,020,000
In individual possession	130,880,500	83,116,600	91,831,800

From this table it is evident that, mainly as a result of the embittered struggle for collectivization, the Soviet Union lost between 1929 and 1930 almost a quarter of its big-horned cattle, almost a third of its sheep and almost half of its pigs. It is estimated that the pigs, although they declined most severely, will be almost replaced during 1931, owing to the possibilities of quick breeding. In the case of cattle and sheep the recovery will evidently require a longer period of time. The heavy decline in livestock is one of the most striking failures in the realization of the Five-Year Plan, which contemplated a steady increase in the number of livestock. The reduction was perhaps the last big despairing act of the vanishing individualist peasantry — the sort of act that no planning experts could foresee.

That the effects of the decline of livestock will be sharply felt throughout 1931 is indicated by other figures cited in Mr. Grinko's article, indicating that the value of products of animal husbandry, which was 5,475,000,000 rubles in 1930, will be 4,638,000,000 rubles in 1931, while the value of the marketable surplus of such products will decline from 1,390,000,000 rubles to 1,237,000,000 rubles. Relief from the present acute shortage of meat, dairy products, eggs, etc., will apparently only begin to be felt in 1932.

Communist economic leaders are convinced that such relief is only a matter of time. They contend that the drastic reduction of cattle in 1930 was due to a combination of circumstances that is unlikely to recur; that the backbone of *kulak* resistance is now broken; that new regulations providing for the compensation of collective farm members for property which they bring into the enterprise will exert a deterrent effect on further killing of cattle; that the fodder situation is more favorable. They also point to the success of the grain collective farms as an omen of what may be expected from state cattle ranches and dairy farms when sufficient time has passed to permit the proper organization of the latter. It is quite possible that these arguments will be borne out by facts in a not too distant future. But at least during 1931 the deficiencies in the field of animal husbandry are bound to exert an unfavorable influence on the supply of food and certain kinds of raw material.

Whether it be measured by the number of people affected, by the magnitude of change effected in working habits and in daily life or by the novelty of the new forms introduced, the introduction of state and collective farming on a large scale deserves to rank as the major innovation brought to pass under the Five-Year Plan. Agriculture has always been a stumbling block in the way of socialism. The Social Democratic parties in Europe have collected few votes in rural districts. And, while it is easy enough to envisage the transfer of factories and mines, railroads and public utilities, operated by hired workers and employees, from private to public ownership, it has always been difficult to fit the peasant or farmer into a Marxian scheme of things. He was an owner, even though a small one, and his instinct for private property was strongly developed.

The problem of overcoming the individualism of the peasant and of bringing Russia's millions of little homesteads into some large scale scheme of socialist or cooperative production was too difficult to solve during the first stage of the Russian Revolution, in the period from 1917 until 1921. The proclamation of the New Economic Policy was a compromise, a truce, as events showed, rather than a permanent peace, between the socialist policies of the Soviet Government and the individualist tendencies of the peasantry.

Some pessimistic prophets both inside and outside the Communist Party ranks were inclined to believe that the effort by drastic means to alter the status of the peasants and to remodel agriculture on a socialist basis would end disastrously, with famine and peasant revolts. But the situation in 1929 and 1930 was very much more favorable for a " socialist offensive " against the " capitalist elements " in the Russian village than it was in 1919 and 1920. Ten years ago Russia was torn by civil war; its industrial production had declined almost to the vanishing point under the combined effects of the Great War, the Revolution, intervention and blockade. There were practically no tractors in the country, and no means of procuring any. Even simpler agricultural implements were lacking.

Now, by straining the national resources to the limit and imposing considerable deprivations on the population as consumers, it has proved possible to pour into agriculture a substantial quantity of tractors and other machinery from foreign sources, besides greatly increasing production in Soviet factories. Consequently it has been possible to lay something of an economic foundation for large scale farming by the provision of large agricultural machinery. This foundation will be broadened in the near future as the tractor factory which has been built at Stalingrad begins to produce on a large scale, and as the projected new tractor plants at Cheliabinsk and Kharkov come into operation.

Moreover, the East European peasant is naturally passive and inclined to submit to authority. During the turmoil of civil war, when there was no universally recognized government and hostile armies were fighting all over the country, the peasants organized guerrilla bands and fought in various provinces against the return of the landlords, which was associated with the victories of the Whites, and against the requisitions imposed by the Soviets, when these became too galling. But now the Soviet régime has had a decade of unchallenged existence. Its methods of dealing with opponents are firm and uncompromising. Consequently many peasants who would never have entered collective farms if the matter had been left purely to their free choice did not feel that they could stand out against a new system which the " vlast," or " power," as the peasants often call the Government, was supporting to the limit of its resources. Another factor in the situation is the growing up in Soviet schools and under the influence of such organizations as the Union of Communist Youth of a new generation of peasant youth, less instinctively opposed to such startling novelties as collective farms than their bearded fathers and grandfathers.

The new state and collective forms of agriculture in Russia are no longer experimental; after the experience of the last harvest they are clearly destined to remain and expand. Even in animal husbandry, where the mistakes in the early methods of collectivization and the resistance of the more well-to-do peasants caused such heavy losses, future reconstruction is envisaged along the line of increasing socialization. With its monopolistic control of credit and machinery, the state can mold agriculture almost according to its choice, and a continuation of the present policy over a few years should bring about the almost complete elimination of the individual farmer.

Every new system brings its own new problems, and collective farming is no exception to this rule. One of the most acute immediate difficulties, as the writer found when he visited a number of collective farms last summer, is the shortage of such manufactured products as textiles, clothing, shoes, sugar, tea, etc. He visited the farms before the harvest had been bought up, and perhaps the situation improved to some extent subsequently, because it is a regular feature of Soviet commercial policy to send large quantities of manufactured goods into the villages at harvest time in order to persuade the peasants to part with their grain and other products more readily.

However, it is very doubtful if a satisfactory balance has yet been struck between agricultural output on one side and the supply of manufactured goods for daily consumption on the other. One sign that the former heavily outweighs the latter is the arrangement, in force in a number of districts, that the peasant who sells his grain at the price fixed by the state has the right to spend only 30 or 35% of the money which he has received for this grain (and for which he can produce a receipt from the state or cooperative organization which bought it) on manufactured goods of which there is a shortage. And there is a shortage of almost every important item in the list of manufactured goods.

In an effort to stimulate higher productivity in

state and collective farms the managers of those enterprises, with the support of local Communist groups and nonparty sympathizers, are attempting to extend to agriculture the system of " socialist competition " and "shock brigades " which, as has already been described, has been generally applied in industry. Less spectacular, but perhaps more effective, methods of inducing the peasant to put forth his best efforts in the collective farm would be the provision of an adequate supply of manufactured goods, so that he would be certain of being able to buy an adequate equivalent for his money, and a closer and more accurate adjustment of payment in the collective farms to the amount and quality of work performed by each member. The last principle, to be sure, is accepted, but does not seem as yet to be applied with the certainty and precision which one would find in a factory system of payment.

A problem of longer range is the effect on the peasant's political and general psychology of the grouping of large numbers of peasant households, each formerly intent on its personal interests, in collective farms, where every member must to a greater or less degree be concerned for the welfare of the enterprise as a whole. Will the peasants, when weight of organization is added to weight of

141

numbers, demand as compensation for their lost rights of private ownership equalization with the city workers in such matters as wages, hours of labor, social benefits and recreation and vacation facilities? Already there are warnings against " consuming tendencies " in collective farms. This is a general term of opprobrium for real or alleged efforts to subordinate the interests of the state, or of the collective farm as an enterprise, to the direct interests of the individual peasant members. One method of combatting these " consuming tendencies " is the strengthening of the Communist Party and Young Communist groups in the collective farms. Such groups are bound by strict Party discipline and are expected in time to play the same leading and energizing rôle that they already play in the factories.

The sweep of collective and state farming in the Soviet Union is a matter of national and international significance. It is a landmark in the history of Soviet economic development, because it implies three important results: the breaking of the crisis of stagnation and underproduction that threatened Russian agriculture, especially grain-farming; the bringing of the long stubbornly recalcitrant branch of agriculture into the orbit of planned economic life; and the combination of two momentous changes in the Soviet agrarian system, its mechanization and its socialization.

For the outside world the remaking of Russian farming undoubtedly carries the promise, or the threat, of steadily increasing exports of grain. Of course, a drought may upset the most elaborate mechanization or the best laid plans; but over a term of years it seems almost impossible that the marketable Soviet grain surplus will not substantially increase, if one considers the program of large scale tractor construction within the country, the swelling acreage that is to be planted by the collective farms, and similar factors. The output of other crops such as cotton, sugar beets, oil seeds and flax may increase for the same reason; but these latter products are not likely to be exported in such volume as grain, because the Russian factories still have a great unsatisfied demand for these forms of raw material.

CHAPTER IV

PLANNED ECONOMIC LIFE: RESULTS AND PROSPECTS

THE Five-Year Plan has now run more than half of its appointed course, if one reckons according to the new date for the completion of the plan, — the end of 1932. What have been the results, the successes and the failures up to the present time? Answers to this question may vary widely, depending upon what standards of success and what economic measuring rods are applied. In drawing up a balance sheet of the Five-Year Plan the writer would be inclined to list on the credit side, in the following order of importance, these main favorable items:

(1) The drawing of a quarter of the peasant homesteads into collective farms and the obtaining of substantially improved crop yields of grain, cotton and sugar beets, mainly as a result of the

widespread introduction of state and collective farming.

(2) The growth at the rate of 24 or 25% a year of the output of the state industries, combined with the progress and, in some cases, the completion, of some huge and many medium-sized industrial and mining plants.

(3) The abolition of nonpolitical unemployment.

On the negative side the writer would set down, again in the order of relative importance, the following developments:

(1) The deterioration of living standards, especially in the towns, as a result of the diminished food supply and the acute shortage of many manufactured goods.

(2) The failure of qualitative improvements in industry to match quantitative gains, and the failure, in some cases, of various branches of economic life to keep in step with each other.

(3) The heavy blow which the cattle and poultry raising and dairying branches of agriculture have received as a result of the widespread destruction of livestock.

If one looks from the past to the future one feels reasonably certain that the quantitative goals of the Five-Year Plan will, in the great majority of cases, be reached and in some cases exceeded by the end of 1932, unless there is some quite unforeseen internal breakdown or external interruption. In the light of past experiences one is apt to be more doubtful about the attainibility, within two years, of the objectives of the Five-Year Plan as regards improved quality of output and a standard of living that should be appreciably better than that of 1927-28.

The measure of success which planned economic life will bring in the Soviet Union depends in no small degree upon two factors which are rather imponderable and not easily reduced to columns of statistics. The first of these is the physical and psychological ability of the masses to stand the strain which has been placed upon them and to achieve higher and higher productivity until the conditions of the supply of food and manufactured goods take a decisive turn for the better. The second is the degree to which the real effectiveness of Soviet production can be made to approximate its imposing numerical gains. To put the matter more concretely, when can it be assumed that 1,000,000 tons of Soviet steel will prove as durable and as serviceable in rails or in construction projects as 1,000,000 tons of American or German or British steel? When will 10,000 tractors, produced by the " Red Putilov " works in Leningrad or by the new plants in Stalingrad or Cheliabinsk do as much work with as little breakage as the same number of tractors imported from America? It is by such tests, rather than by mere figures of physical growth of production, that the effectiveness of the Soviet economic system must increasingly be measured.

Whatever may be the reactions of an outside observer, the leading figures in the Communist Party and the Soviet Government are not inclined to admit that the difficulties and setbacks which have been encountered in the execution of the Five-Year Plan weigh seriously in the balance against the tremendous achievements to which they lay claim. Their attitude is more understandable if one considers that their test of appraisal is progress toward the building up of socialism. An authoritative definition of socialism in this connection was given by Stalin, in his report before the enlarged plenary session of the Executive Committee of the Communist International on December 7, 1926 : [1]

We won the dictatorship of the proletariat and thereby created the political basis for the movement forward to

[1] Cited by N. Atan, in an article in *Rabochaya Moskva* for January 12, 1931.

147

socialism. Can we create with our own forces the economic basis of socialism, a new economic foundation, necessary for the building up of socialism? Wherein is the economic basis and economic substance of socialism? Is it to establish a " paradise on earth " and general satisfaction? No, it is not in this. That is a conception of the substance of socialism that belongs to the man in the street, to the petty bourgeois. To create an economic basis for socialism means to unite agriculture with socialist industry in one integral economic system, to subordinate agriculture to the guidance of socialist industry, to establish relations between city and village on the basis of direct exchange of products of industry and of agriculture, to close and liquidate all those channels with the aid of which classes and, above all, capital are born, to create in the end such conditions of production and distribution as will lead directly to the annihilation of classes.

That great progress has been made toward socialism, as covered by this definition, during the last two years, is undeniable. Certainly the channels of private trade have been more and more closed and liquidated, while the small individual land holdings of the peasantry are being more and more swallowed up in collective farms. *Pravda* of December 21, 1930, states that the socialist section now embraces 62% of all the basic capital of national economic life. This proportion will be further increased if the project of collectivizing at least 50% of the peasant holdings by the end of 1931 is carried out. The year 1931, with its program of a 45% increase in industrial production and a doubling of the percentage of collectivization in agriculture, is habitually referred to as the year when the foundation of socialism will be completed in the Soviet Union. This point was emphasized in a speech by a member of the Political Bureau of the Communist Party Central Committee, L. M. Kaganovich, in a speech delivered before Moscow Party members on December 24, 1930,[1] from which the following passages may be cited:

> In this year we complete the building of the foundation of socialist economic life. The decisive fact is that petty bourgeois elemental economic tendencies already do not predominate in our country. In 1931 more than half of the peasant households in the whole Soviet Union and 80% of the homesteads in the basic grain regions will be united in collective farms. Consequently, the predominant form of organization also in the village will be socialist. If the economic life of the country as a whole is taken, we will have an overwhelming predominance of the socialist section.

The Communist leaders feel that, besides laying the foundation of a socialist economic system, they are already carrying out Lenin's injunction " to overtake and outstrip the leading capitalist countries." The columns of the Soviet press abound in articles contrasting the intensified industrial construction in the Soviet Union with the

[1] Published in *Rabochaya Moskva* for December 30, 1930.

149

decline of production which was observed in many foreign lands in connection with the world depression of 1930. The Soviet challenge to the " capitalist " world was phrased in the following terms by V. V. Kuibishev in the course of a speech which he delivered at a session of the Soviet Central Executive Committee on January 5, 1931:

Our country with its planned socialist system of administering economic life does not and will not know crises. We do not fear overproduction because all the surplus production, created by the labor of the workers, in the socialist state increases the well-being of the toilers. The extension of production can not with us become a cause of the misfortunes into which the workers of the capitalist world fall. We can have no overproduction, because the welfare of the workers and wages grow with us. With them crisis is inevitable, because crisis reflects the very structure of the capitalist order. Such is the nature of capitalism, such is the nature of that system which is opposed to us. High rates of progress are inaccessible to capitalism, because the unavoidable crises are reflected destructively on the productive forces of the country. Capitalism will never obtain such high rates of progress as ours because there no planned organized economic system exists. Thanks to our organized economic system we can exploit all possibilities in every individual branch of economic life. . . .

Going ahead at high rates of speed, we will more and more overtake capitalist countries. The slogan " to overtake and outstrip " already becomes a reality in a number of branches of economic life and industry. Thus, we overtook England in pig iron in 1929, despite the fact that in 1929 British production was still rising. We overtook France in steel

150

in 1928, despite the fact that France in 1927 considerably exceeded our manufacture of steel. Much the same thing occurred in regard to coal. If we fulfill our coal program for 1931 we will more than three times exceed the coal output of Belgium,[1] that little Belgium which quite recently exceeded us by one and a half times, and we will leave far behind France, which in 1926 was ahead of us by more than two times.

So the race has begun. We are still far from the level of the leading capitalist countries. The level of our production, of the development of our economic life is still extremely low. But we will reach the goal sooner than the capitalist world, because for us work the great forces of history, the pitiless logic of class war, because for us is the working class of our country and of the whole world — the class which conquers, the class which will overthrow capitalism and establish the socialist economic system in the whole world.

The year 1931, like the two years which have preceded it, will be difficult and strenuous. The high goals which have been set — the 45% increase in industrial output and, still more, perhaps, the 28% increase in labor productivity and the 10% reduction in production costs — will not be achieved without a struggle. The situation is

[1] [The coal production of the Soviet Union for 1921 (October, 1920–September, 1921) was 8,520,000 metric tons compared with Belgium's 21,750,000. The production of Belgium for the calendar year and of the Soviet Union for the fiscal year in recent periods has been:

Belgium		Soviet Union	
1927	27,540,000	1926–27	32,018,000
1928	27,543,000	1927–28	35,241,200
1929	26,928,000	1928–29	39,658,700
1930	27,408,000	1929–30	46,650,900
		1931 (program)	83,600,000
			Editor]

complicated by the fact that the country's reserves of skilled labor are already exhausted, so that the 700,000 new manual workers who will be required in industry will have to be drawn largely from classes without previous experience in large scale industry. Another difficult task, if precedents count for anything, is the projected effort to complete the year without issuing new currency.

A certain increase of production is guaranteed by the fact that a number of big new plants will come partially or wholly into operation during 1931. Among the plants which are supposed to come into full operation are the Nizhni Novgorod automobile plant, with its annual capacity of 140,000 automobiles and trucks, the Kharkov tractor factory, with a capacity of 50,000 tractors a year, the Saratov combine plant, capable of turning out 20,000 combines a year, the Berezinkovsky chemical factory, which is supposed to produce 300,000 tons of highly concentrated fertilizers for agriculture, and a Ural copper plant, which is designed to produce 10,000 or 12,000 tons of copper a year. Among those which will be partially launched are the Magnitogorsk and Kuznetzk plants, of which the former is expected ultimately to produce 4,000,000 and the latter 1,100,000 tons of pig iron annually, the Siberian combine plant and the large Ural machine building works, designed ultimately to yield 150,000 tons of output a year.

Because of the iron discipline which reigns within the Communist Party (the sole legal political organization in the Soviet Union), there can be little openly expressed dissent from the program of high-speed industrialization of the country and collectivization of agriculture which has been in operation during the last two years. Soon after the exclusion from the Party of the Trotzkyists,[1] a " right " opposition, headed by Premier A. I. Rykov, the head of the Trade Union Council, Mikhail Tomsky, and the editor of the Communist Party central organ, *Pravda*, Nikolai Bukharin began to make itself felt. Although little public discussion is possible, in view of the political conditions which prevail in the Soviet Union, it was generally understood that the right oppositionists believed that industrialization was being pushed too fast, and that it also favored a slower pace of collectivization and more consideration for the interests of the individual peasants. Stronger and stronger disciplinary measures were taken against right oppositionists and in November, 1929, Rykov, Tomsky and Bukharin signed a document

[1] See p. 13.

recanting their views. They have now all been removed from their former influential posts, Bukharin and Tomsky early in 1929 and Rykov in December, 1930.

A more recent dissident group developed under the leadership of the ex-premier of the Russian Soviet Republic, S. I. Sirtsov, and a prominent Party official in the Trans-Caucasus, Lominadze. The official Party press accused Sirtsov and Lominadze of attempting to cover up " right ideas" with "left phrases." One knows the program of the Sirtsov-Lominadze group largely from the denunciations which have been launched against it, because no group of political dissidents in the Soviet Union, either within or without the Communist Party, enjoys much chance of publicly advocating its views.

Sirtsov apparently suggested that, instead of concentrating on rapid quantitative increase in industrial production, more attention should be paid to correcting mistakes and bolstering up weak spots in the industrial mechanism. Other statements attributed to him are that the living standards of the workers have deteriorated, that the Soviet bureaucracy is functioning worse and not better than formerly, and that many of the special devices employed to stimulate improve-

154

ment in the work of the factories and cooperative stores, such as the organization of "shock brigades," the practice of "socialist competition" between factories and institutions, the continual inspection of factories by delegations from others, and the creation of a multitude of informal control organs to supervise distribution in the cooperative stores, have brought more confusion and dislocation than positive benefit. Avowed sympathizers with Sirtsov and Lominadze, like followers of Trotzky or of the right opposition, are subject to exclusion from the Communist Party.

The influence of the Five-Year Plan has extended far beyond the purely economic sphere. To a greater or less degree it has affected every phase of Russian life. The capacity of the Russian masses to stand the strain and deprivations which are being imposed on them can not properly be gaged if it is not borne in mind that the Soviet Government has created what is perhaps the greatest propaganda machine in history, and has placed before this machine as its first task the continual exposition, advocacy and glorification of the Five-Year Plan.

Every Soviet newspaper to-day is filled with reports from the main "economic front," and from the numerous minor " fronts " into which it is subdivided — the coal front, the metal front, the transport front, the lumber front, etc. Columns of space are devoted to descriptions of the socialist competitions between factories. The enormous amount of space devoted to news on economic subjects which in other countries would be restricted to trade journals or to the business sections of newspapers, corresponds with the high proportion of the Soviet national income which is directed through various channels into industrial construction.

The Moscow theater to-day might almost be called the theater of the Five-Year Plan. An extraordinary number of new plays, of varying degrees of interest and artistic skill, attempt to depict the struggles and problems of the present era of industrialization. The same thing may be said of art, much of the new painting and sculpture being devoted to the depiction of new building and farm and factory processes. One can not escape the all-pervading influence of the Five-Year Plan even in the moving picture theater. A performance the writer recently attended began with a lusty propaganda performance intitled " The Party Calls," which consisted of scenes filmed at various centers of construction, such as Magnitogorsk, Dnieprstroi, etc. It ended with an appeal to bend redoubled efforts for the achievement of the tasks marked out for the third decisive year of the plan and gave derisive pictures of the absentee from work with the vodka bottle which explained his " desertion from the labor front," and of the " flier " who moves from one factory to another. There was an almost equally heavy dose of industrialization propaganda in the regular film which followed. Here the heroine was a Young Communist working girl and the villain was another Young Communist, whose sin was not that he enticed her into a more or less regularized union, but that he persuaded her to give up working in the factory. In the end her proletarian conscience wins the day, and she returns to her machine amid the applause of her fellow-workers.

The school, the trade union, the workers' club, the radio and a host of similar agencies are all making contributions to the huge campaign of agitation for the Five-Year Plan. A multi-colored electrical sign over the entrance to the chief Moscow post and telegraph office shows the figure five being crossed out and replaced by four, as a symbol of the acceleration of the plan. The concentrated effort to mobilize popular sentiment for the projects of industrialization closely corresponds with the centralized mobilization of the resources of the country for the realization of the plan.

Enthusiastic Communists in the Soviet Union and apprehensive anti-Communists in foreign countries sometimes assume that the success of the Five-Year Plan will deal a severe, and possibly mortal, blow to the " capitalist " system in the rest of the world. One can understand the psychological motives which may impel the Communist leaders to strengthen the morale of the Russian masses by attempting to convince them that as a result of their present-day hardships a tremendous blow is being struck for the world revolution. But when one resorts to sober analysis there seems no economic reason why the fulfilment of the present Five-Year Plan, or of several five-year plans (for it should always be emphasized that not the five years, but the plan is the important element in the Soviet scheme of industrial organization), should violently upset the political, economic and social order in other countries. This is not to say, of course, that the outside world will not be well advised to study closely and impartially the gigantic Soviet economic experiment, and to profit by such lessons as may be learned from it. But the theory, whether it is advanced in Soviet or in foreign circles, that the industrialization of the Soviet Union necessarily means the breakdown of the private capitalist system all over the world, seems to lack a solid factual foundation.

Formidable pictures are sometimes painted of the Soviet's flooding the world with the cheap products of its new factories. As a matter of fact, in no country in the world is the potential internal market so large, so hungry and so inexhaustible as in the Union itself. Under any settled system of government a country endowed with the Soviet Union's natural resources and industrial possibilities could not be excluded from the world's markets; nor would it be for the advantage of the rest of the world if it were excluded. As for the menace of undercutting all other countries in the matter of prices, the Soviet Union to-day is not a large scale exporter of manufactured goods of any kind; and is not likely to become one until the " qualitative indices " of its industries are substantially improved. In exporting grain, lumber, oil, furs, manganese and other raw material and agricultural products, the Soviet Union is merely following in the footsteps of prewar Russia and has not yet attained prewar Russia's share in world trade.

The belief is sometimes expressed, with hope by the Communists, with fear by anti-Communists, that the success of the Five-Year Plan will raise the prestige of communism all over the world and constitute an indirect incitement to revolution. But, as the writer has attempted to show, the success of the plan is subject to certain reservations and qualifications. If there has been an overfulfilment as regards industrial output there has been an underfulfilment as regards the supply of meat, milk and eggs to the population, and the problem of quality also remains to be solved. No one who knows from personal observation how difficult life still is for the worker in the factory and the peasant in the collective farm with respect to such fundamental things as food and clothing, is likely to envisage a very speedy rise in the Soviet standard of living to a point where it would excite the envy of the majority of the people in Western Europe and America. It may be that two or three years will have to elapse before foodstuffs can be bought as freely as was the case in 1926 or 1927. And when that point had been reached a stupendous amount of production of all kinds, perhaps the equivalent of two or three more five-year plans, would be necessary before there could be much question of "overtaking and outstripping the leading capitalist countries." Before that ideal could be achieved an almost incalculable quantity of automobiles, telephone lines, furniture, clothing, household utensils and other manufactured articles would have to be thrown on the market. The field for improvement in road building, sanitation, medical aid, etc., is also still very great.

Even if planned economic life should ultimately bring great prosperity to the Soviet Union this would not mean, as has sometimes been hastily assumed, some kind of catastrophic disaster for countries with different political, economic and social systems. An increase of prosperity and purchasing power in the Soviet Union would be beneficial, rather than otherwise, to the rest of the world. Experience would tend to show that it is not the prosperous countries, but rather the backward and poverty-stricken lands which clog and delay the progress of world economic life as a whole.

One can scarcely look back over the history of the last two years in the Soviet Union without feeling that the adoption of the 1928–1933 Five-Year Plan was an event of great and increasing importance. It has meant a tremendous concentration and straining of national effort for the achievement of exceedingly difficult and ambitious economic problems. It involved the cutting, in very summary fashion, of many Gordian knots of

Soviet economic life during the period of the New Economic Policy. The "liquidation of the *kulaks* as a class," for instance, seems to have dealt a crushing, if not as yet a completely fatal, blow to the individual peasant proprietor, who five years ago seemed such an insuperable stumbling block in the way of the complete realization of socialism.

The carrying out of the Five-Year Plan has changed the visible face of the Soviet Union more than the original Bolshevik Revolution had changed the prewar Russia. The little strips and patches, so characteristic of the peasant homestead method of farming in Russia, have disappeared over wide expanses of territory, and have been replaced by great unbroken stretches of steppe, the property of a state or collective farm. One can scarcely visit any provincial town without finding some signs of new building. Even the calendar, the most conservative of human institutions, has been swept away to some extent. Under the new system, by which factories and offices work continuously,[1] the employees receiving one free day in every five, people tend completely to forget the days of the week: the average Russian to-day is puzzled if one asks him

[1] See further "The Continuous Working Week in Soviet Russia," *International Labour Review*, XXIII, p. 157.

whether it is Tuesday, Thursday or Saturday. The bare shelves of many of the stores, the terrific crowding whenever there is an unrestricted sale of manufactured goods, the food booklets with their numerous coupons permitting holders to buy in cooperative stores limited amounts of bread, meat, sugar, etc., are all signs of the price which the country is paying for its rapid industrialization.

We are still too close to the Soviet new economic era which was ushered in by the Five-Year Plan to judge its significance with any degree of finality. When one looks back on this hard, strained, driving, intense period from a perspective of ten or twenty years, one will be in a better position to judge which of the varied and sometimes contradictory phenomena which strike the attention of the observer to-day were of permanent and which were of transitory significance.

It is already possible, however, to say that the Soviet Union has embarked on a " newest economic policy " of the greatest importance, first, for itself, second, for the rest of the world, which can not help seeing and, to a certain extent, being influenced by Russian developments. There can no longer be any reasonable expectation that the Soviet Union will revert to " capitalism." A country which rivals America in natural resources,

163

in combined potentialities of industrial and agricultural development, has definitely broken with the traditional economic system and has set about the task of organizing its economic life on socialist lines. As Kuibishev said, the race between the " capitalist " and " socialist " economic systems has begun.

APPENDICES

APPENDIX I

Resolution of the Fifth Congress of Soviets, Moscow, May 28, 1929 [1]

THE FIVE-YEAR PLAN OF ECONOMIC DEVELOPMENT

Having heard the reports of Comrades G. M. Krzhizhanovsky and V. V. Kuibishev, the Fifth All-Union Congress of Soviets approves the Five-Year Plan of national economic upbuilding of the Soviet Union, approved by the Government, and decides:

1. To note that the enormous advantages of the Soviet economic system and the correct economic policy of the Soviet power, based on the firm union of the working class with the poor and middle class layers of the village, guaranteed within a short time the reestablishment of the economic life of the Soviet Union above the prewar level and brought the country on the road of socialist reconstruction. The Five-Year Plan proposed by the Government, being a developed program of socialist reconstruction of economic life, corresponds with the general course of the Soviet power toward the industrialization of the Soviet Union, toward the socialist reconstruction of the village, toward the overcoming of capitalist, and the consequent strengthening of socialist, elements in the economic order of the country, and toward the raising of the defensive capacity of the Soviet Union.

At the same time the Congress observes with satisfaction

[1] Translated from Bulletin No. 22 of the Decisions of the Congress, p. 9–14.

167

the decisive economic and cultural upswing of the backward regions and nationalities of the Soviet Union, contemplated by the Five-Year Plan.

2. The Congress approves the power provisions of the Five-Year Plan and the broad program of electrification which lies at its base. This program contemplates the increase of the capacity of the regional electrical stations from 500,000 kilowatts at the beginning to 3,200,000 kilowatts at the end of the Five-Year Plan. In full accordance with the Eighth Congress of Soviets of the Russian Socialist Federative Soviet Republic, which in 1920, upon the initiative of Comrade Lenin, confirmed a plan of electrification, the Congress considers that the problems of building and extending 42 regional electrical stations and of constructing the biggest industrial combination plants around powerful electrical stations — problems which are outlined by the Five-Year Plan — are the decisive prerequisite for the realization of the scheme of reconstruction of the national economic life, and for the successful accomplishment of the slogan proclaimed by the Communist Party: "To overtake and outstirp the leading capitalist countries in technique and economic organization." The Congress observes that the program of socialist industrialization projected in the Five-Year Plan, which finds expression in the growth of industrial production by more than two and a half times, in the strengthening of the positions of heavy industry and in the scope of capital building, defined for industry at 16,400,000,000 rubles for the five-year period, is in full harmony with the power provisions of the plan, with the idea of strengthening the chemical industries of the country and with the problems of reconstructing all branches of economic life which are set down by the plan.

The Congress commends to the special attention and observation of the Government those productive tasks for the end of the Five-Year Plan which are contemplated in the plan and which are decisive for the socialist industrialization of the country: the output of 22,000,000,000 kilowatt-hours of electrical energy, 75,000,000 tons of coal, 22,000,000 tons of oil, and 10,000,000 tons of pig iron; strong development of the chemical industry of the whole country, and especially the production of more than 8,000,000 tons of mineral fertilizers; general machine building of an annual value of 2,000,000,000 rubles; agricultural machinery building to the value of 610,000,000 rubles; and the output of 53,000 tractors annually.

In regard to the strengthening of the defensive capacity of the Soviet Union the Congress commissions the Government, in executing the Five-Year Plan, to take concrete measures guaranteeing the development of those branches of economic life which are inseparably connected with the defensive capacity of the country.

3. The Congress especially approves the broad program of outliving the backwardness of agriculture indicated by the Five-Year Plan, the increase of its productive forces in full harmony with the sweeping industrial development of the country, the decisive crushing of the *kulak* top layers of the village, and the transition to mass socialization of agricultural production (creation of state and collective farms, and machine-tractor stations; intensification of cooperation and the contracting of crops, etc.). Only this can assure the many millions of poor and middle class peasants access to the road of economic upswing, and socialist reconstruction of the individual peasant farm.

Powerful support by the quickly growing socialist industry, new forms of productive cooperation of city and village, the experience of big mechanized farms, the broad application of machines and chemical fertilizers, the wide development of agricultural sciences, stimulation of the growth of individual farms, ever broader understanding by the toiling peasantry of the direct advantages from passing to the road of mass collectivization and cooperation on the basis of big-machine technique, — only this road guarantees the swift outliving of the age-old backwardness of peasant farming and the progressive increase of its productive forces.

The Congress summons the many millions of poor and middle class peasants decisively to support the plan of developing agriculture which has been indicated by the Communist Party and the Soviet power, and by powerful toiling cooperation to hasten the solution of the great problems of socialist reconstruction of the village.

4. The Congress notes the broad program of transport construction projected by the Five-Year Plan. This plan is based on large scale reconstruction of railroad transport, on new railroad building, guaranteeing the extension of the railroad lines from 76,000 kilometers at the beginning to 92,000 kilometers at the end of the Five-Year Plan, and on the decisive overcoming of the lack of roads by the widespread building of paved and wagon roads, and on the substantial development of new forms of transport (motor and aviation).

Simultaneously, the Congress commissions the Government to reexamine the program of works on water transport designated in the Five-Year Plan in order to extend these works further, both by improving service on the existing routes and by further extension of the system of river routes, with a corresponding development of shipbuilding.

Appraising the extreme inadequacy of existing routes of communication in relation to the gigantic distances of the country, and the most important problems of drawing new regions into the sphere of commercial exchange, the Congress considers the program of transport construction a minimum task, and makes it obligatory for the Government in the course of the fulfilment of the Five-Year Plan to exploit all possibilities for exceeding this program.

The Congress also makes it obligatory for all local organs of the Soviet power, and summons all social organizations, to concentrate their efforts on the struggle with lack of roads, which delays our economic development.

5. The solution of the great building and productive problems, set by the Five-Year Plan, can be accomplished only on condition that there is a great growth of labor productivity, that there is a considerable enhancement of the harvest yield, that there is a great reduction in the costs of industrial production, building and transport services — i. e., on condition that there is a great improvement in the qualitative indices of national economic life, guaranteeing to the country indispensable capital accumulation, indispensable reserves of food and indispensable economy in the expenditure of money, raw material, supplies and fuel. Fully approving the tasks indicated in this direction by the Five-Year Plan, the Congress directs the attention of the Government to the necessity of creating by means of a series of measures conditions which would guarantee not only the full realization of the qualitative indices which are indicated and which determine the fate of the national economic plan, but also, if possible, the exceeding of these indices. Improvement of the technical equipment of labor, the toiling enthusiasm of the masses, the consolidation of enthusiastic, conscious socialist discipline, better organization of economic management, decisive struggle with bureaucratism, broadest development of self-criticism, broadest development of socialist competition among factories, railroads, workshops, state and collective farms, separate villages and whole regions in the fulfilment of the great tasks of socialist construction, — all this, taken together, must insure such a growth of labor productivity in the country of the Soviets as would be un-

attainable in capitalist society. The Congress turns to the broad masses of workers and peasants, to technical experts, to educational and medical workers, etc., with an appeal to help by their activity, initiative and toiling discipline the accomplishment of these tasks which are set by the plan.

6. The Congress approves the growth in numbers of the labor force employed in industry and the considerable reduction of unemployment contemplated by the plan, with the simultaneous basic reconstruction and rationalization of industry, the placing of all industrial and transport workers on the seven-hour working day, the substantial increase of real wages and of the welfare of the broad toiling masses of the peasant population, the gradual liquidation of the material and cultural distinction between city and village. The Congress sees in this the difference, in principle, between socialist reconstruction and the ways of capitalist rationalization of production, which plunge the broad masses of the toilers into chronic unemployment and hopeless need.

The Congress commissions the Government to take all measures which are necessary for the complete achievement of the above mentioned tasks of the Five-Year Plan in improving the welfare of the toiling masses.

7. Observing that the Five-Year Plan has raised problems connected with improved education of the masses, and emphasizing the fact that a decisive and general educational improvement in the country, the preparation of trained experts for all branches of economic life and full use of the latest achievements of world science and technique are indispensable conditions for the successful achievement of the Five-Year Plan, the Congress commissions the Government by appropriate measures to guarantee the following reforms, indicated by the plan: radical improvement of the conditions of labor in undertakings and extension of the program of social insurance; transition to general compulsory education

of children; decisive struggle with illiteracy; extension of the school system; further development of public halls, clubs, nurseries, restaurants, reading rooms, etc.; broad development of technical and economic education; widely planned development of scientific investigating institutes and work; preparation of new and rational use and retraining of existing experts of all professions and grades; invitation of the best foreign specialists; broad development of literature in the languages of all the peoples of the Soviet Union; widespread development of the motion picture and the radio, and accomplishment of other educational measures designated by the Five-Year Plan and necessary for the socialist reconstruction of economic life.

The Congress especially emphasizes the general intensification of the struggle with the housing need and the obligatory fulfilment of the program of housing construction and municipal improvements projected by the Five-Year Plan.

The Congress calls all public organizations, trade unions, cooperatives, etc., to contribute by their initiative to the solution of the enormous problems of educational upbuilding in the country.

8. The Congress approves the financial program indicated in the Five-Year Plan, based upon the raising of the buying power of the *chervonetz* (Soviet ruble), the accumulation of considerable foreign currency reserves and the widespread mobilization of the people's resources for the needs of economic and educational construction. The Congress commissions the Government and all organs of the Soviet power to work constantly for the further strengthening of the régime of economy in the expenditure of the people's resources, and of firm financial discipline, since it is only under these conditions that the Soviet country can achieve big industrial building which is unparalleled in history.

9. The Congress notes with satisfaction that the Five-Year Plan of economic life designates a strong growth of the share of the socialized section in all the basic funds of the country, the inclusion in cooperatives, in complete agreement with the cooperative plan of Lenin, of 54% of the handicraft industry and 85% of the peasant households, still greater inclusion of the working class in cooperatives, widespread development of the socialized section in agriculture (state and collective farms), which must embrace more than 20,000,000 of the peasant population and guarantee about 43% of the marketable grain by the end of the Five-Year Plan. All this must give a smashing blow to the capitalist elements and guarantee the genuine triumph of socialist forms in the economic system of the Soviet Union.

10. The realization of the enormous economic tasks indicated by the plan demands the strained effort of the whole state and economic apparatus of the country.

Under these conditions of developed socialist construction in city and village, the revivification and strengthening of the lower organs of Soviet power, the Soviets and their executive committees, and also the work of these organs in carrying out the measures which proceed from the Five-Year Plan of economic development acquire special significance. Therefore, the Fifth Congress of Soviets of the Soviet Union instructs the Soviet Government to turn serious attention to the provision of the lower organs of authority with necessary material resources and with experienced officials, drawn from the ranks of workers, farm laborers and poor and middle class peasants, and to the further planned development of the lower state apparatus, drawing into its work new millions of toilers, bringing it closer to the population and vigorously rooting out any kind of bureaucratic distortions in it.

11. The toilers of the Soviet Union, under the leadership

of the Communist Party and the Soviet power, moved along the great road of victorious civil war and restoration of the economic life which was destroyed by war and capitalist intervention — the road of struggle and building, along which they accumulated vast economic experience and put forward new trained leaders of the economic life of the country. The Five-Year Plan of economic development, which is a testimonial and result of this accumulated experience of planned guidance of the national economic life, along with this opens up new possibilities and demands the quickest decision of the problems of organization, which acquire exceptional importance for guaranteeing the socialist reconstruction of economic life.

The Congress expresses its firm confidence that, notwithstanding the prophecies of enemies and the waverings of the timid, the toilers of the Soviet Union will overcome the difficulties which stand before them and, after smashing the resistance of the hostile capitalist forces, will victoriously solve the great problems of socialist construction.

*President of the Fifth Congress of Soviets of
the Soviet Union*
M. KALININ

*Secretary of the Fifth Congress of Soviets of
the Soviet Union*
A. YENUKIDZE

Moscow,
May 28, 1929.

APPENDIX II

Introduction to the Five-Year Plan

[Translated from *Pyatiletni Plan: Narodno-Khozyaistvennovo Stroyitelstva S.S.S.R.* (The Five-Year Plan of National Economic Construction of the Soviet Union), I, 9–13.[1]]

1. BASIC PROPOSITIONS

The 15th Congress of the All-Union Communist Party [2] gave exhaustive political and economic directions for the construction of a Five-Year Plan of national economic life, proceeding from the general course toward the industrialization of the Soviet Union, toward the socialist reorganization of the village, toward the overcoming of the capitalist, and the consequent strengthening of socialist, elements in the economic system of the country. Subsequent plenary sessions of the Communist Party Central Committee, on the one hand, and a number of governmental acts on the other (the decree of the Central Executive Committee of the Soviet Union about harvest yield) developed and made more concrete the instructions of the 15th Congress concerning means of developing the productive forces of the country and concerning problems of economic construction in the immediate future. It has been the duty of the State Planning Commission of the Soviet Union and of the whole system of planning organizations to translate these general political and economic propositions and instructions into the language of concrete economic and technical-economic calculations, and to work them over into a plan of economic construction for the ensuing five-year period. The present report on the Five-Year Plan of national economic life is an attempt to solve this problem.

---

[1] *Cf. The Soviet Union Looks Ahead*, Chap. I.

[2] December 2–19, 1927.

2. Observations About Organization and Method

The proposed Five-Year Plan in its measures of projected growth of material production, capital investments and qualitative indices considerably exceeds the calculations of all former projects. At its basis lie the recently accumulated experience of the first years of the reconstruction period, indicating possibilities which were formerly not appraised, and a certain change in the character and nature of the work for the Five-Year Plan. In harmony with the directions of the 15th Party Congress as to giving the work of the Five-Year Plan a broader social character, and also for the purpose of obtaining more diverse scientific expert opinion concerning the most important elements of the plan, the State Planning Commission in the course of its work on the Five-Year Plan held special conferences, attended by the most prominent representatives of science and of practical experience on such questions as metallurgy and machine construction, reconstruction of agriculture, reorganization of transport, the chemical, lumber, wood-chemical and textile industries, minor industry, cooperative organization, the training of skilled workers and specialists in the country and local economic administration.

By utilizing these conferences and also the extensive labors of a number of Commissariats, especially the Supreme Economic Council and the Commissariat for Transport, it was possible to create a sufficiently concrete program (with definition of objectives, regions and time limits) of new building, and also a program of reconstruction and rationalization in the decisive branches of economic life. On this program are based all the projected rates of quantitative and qualitative growth. From the methodological standpoint this made it possible to renounce the method of assumption (extrapolation), to which it was unavoidably necessary to resort in previous stages of prospective planning and which led to the nonappraisal of potential rates of our development and construction.

Along with this the State Planning Commission carried out special conferences with the officials of the most important economic regions of the country, in the course of which, in conjunction with these local authorities, the actual resources and possibilities of each of the regions were weighed, from the standpoint both of the general national problems falling to its share and of its specific characteristics and needs. The work of these regional conferences makes it possible for the first time to present the most important elements of the Five-Year Plan in so far as they affect the regions, thereby revealing the general lines of redistribution of productive forces between the regions and those special problems of developing the backward regions which were especially indicated in the decisions of the 15th Congress.

Finally, in the latest work on the Five-Year Plan it proved possible to throw somewhat more light on a number of such synthetic problems as the national income, the processes of socialization, the balance of the country as regards mechanical power, etc.

The work on the Five-Year Plan up to the present time is not finally completed and therefore further exploration will require supplementary exposition. The basic conclusions, however, are not subject to any serious changes on this account.

3. About the Two Variations of the Plan

The State Planning Commission assumes the necessity of preparing the Five-Year National Economic Plan in two variants. In analyzing the problem of the variants, it is necessary above all to emphasize categorically the unity of the economic course and of the economic program in both. The problems of industrialization and socialization are of

178

determining importance in both variants. The development of the socialized section in agriculture is planned in almost equal dimensions for the two variants. In view of its special importance, this matter is to be forced with maximum speed for the next five years. The distribution of the national income in general and especially the proportion of the share of the proletariat to the total income of the population, in principle, follow the same lines in both variants.

The distinction between the minimum and maximum variants, which have the same economic course, may be summarized as follows. The minimum variant reckons with:

(a) The possibility of a partial crop failure in the course of the Five-Year Plan.

(b) Approximately the present type of relations with world economic life (especially in the sense of the increase of long-term credits, the growth of which is planned at a rate characteristic for the last years).

(c) A relatively slower realization of high qualitative standards in economic life in general and in agriculture in particular.

(d) A greater relative weight of the defense program on the minimum variant, in view of the fact that it is almost identical for both variants.

On the other hand the maximum variant reckons with:

(a) The absence of any serious crop failure in the course of the Five-Year Plan.

(b) Considerably broader economic ties with world economic life, both as a result of the existence of greater export resources within the country (complete realization of the decree of the Soviet Central Executive Committee concerning harvest yield), and especially as a result of a considerably swifter growth of foreign long-term credits even in the first years of the Five-Year Plan.

(c) A sharp upturn in the qualitative indices in economic development during the next two years (cost of production, harvest yield, etc.).

(d) A smaller relative weight of expenditures on defense in the general economic system.

Thus, the movement of our economic development during the next five years, according to one of these variants, may be conditioned both upon a series of outside factors (harvest failure, inadequacy of long-term foreign credits), and upon the degree of our success in the most difficult matter of realizing high qualitative standards (cost of production, harvest yield). In accordance with these considerations the minimum variant may be regarded as a kind of guaranteed minimum within the maximum variant, unity being maintained between the economic programs of the two. The difference between them is calculated, approximately, at 20% (a number of indices remaining identical), — i. e., approximately, at a year's period of development. In other words the program (maximum), which under certain conditions we can accomplish within five years, under the less favorable conditions characteristic of the minimum variant will be stretched out, approximately, over six years. The framing of the Five-Year National Economic Plan in two variants, in view of all the difficulty of this matter, must assure greater maneuvering possibilities in the annual economic plans, and greater preparedness for the overcoming of those enormous difficulties which stand in the way of the achievement of the five-year program of economic construction.

APPENDIX III

Manifesto of the Communist Party Central Committee

REGARDING THE APPROACHING THIRD YEAR OF THE FIVE-YEAR PLAN [1]

To All Party, Economic, Trade-union and Young Communist Organizations:

Within a month begins the new economic year — the third year of the Five-Year Plan. This approaching year puts forward a number of the most complicated and responsible economic and political problems. It has decisive significance for the fulfilment of the Five-Year Plan in four years and must guarantee the passing of not less than half of the peasant households to the socialist road, the road of collectivization.

The third year of the Five-Year Plan means a gigantic new stride in the industrialization of the Soviet Union. The mere growth of production for 1930–31 will be equal to the whole prewar industrial production. In the third year of the Five-Year Plan, along with the finished and already operating Stalingrad tractor factory, the Rostov agricultural machinery factory and other new plants it is necessary to assure the development at full speed of the construction of such huge enterprises as Magnitostroi, on the equipment of which more than 200,000,000 rubles must be expended in one year, Kuznetzkstroi, the Nizhni Novgorod automobile factory, the Kharkov and Cheliabinsk tractor plants, the huge Ural heavy machinery construction factory, the first sections of the great Berezinkovsky and Bobrikovsky chemical combines, the Saratov combine, etc.[2] The overwhelming majority of these factories, which in capacity far

[1] Translated from *Rabochaya Moskva*, September 4, 1930.

[2] Descriptions of the various plants mentioned may be found in the *Economic Review of the Soviet Union*.

181

exceed everything that the country possessed up to this time in the field of the metallurgical, chemical and machinery construction industries, must be started in the course of the third year of the Five-Year Plan — some fully, others in part.

Moreover, in the ensuing year begins the building of such new factories as the Nizhni Tagil and Mariupol metallurgical plants and the Dnieper combine among a number of huge new factories. In 1930–31 we must obtain the first big results in achieving the direction of the 16th Party Congress about the creation of a new coal and metallurgical base in the Soviet Union — the Ural-Kuznetzk combine.

The following decisive figures determine the program of the coming year: 7,500,000 tons of pig iron, 74,500,000 tons of coal, 2,500,000,000 rubles worth of new machines, besides 845,000,000 rubles worth of agricultural machinery and new tractors with a total volume of 745,000 horsepower.

Successes in the development of heavy industry and the growth of the agricultural raw material base (extension of the planted acreage, increased harvest of cotton, sugar beets and a number of other nongrain crops) assure a pace of growth of light industry which will be considerably more rapid than was the case in preceding years. Along with other measures this creates the prerequisite conditions for improving the supply with objects of broad consumption and for mitigating the goods famine.

The realization of this production program demands decisive improvement in the quality of all economic work. All the qualitative indices of the work of industry and, first of all, the indices of cost of production and productivity of labor, must be considerably raised and fulfilled with unconditional accuracy in the course of the year. Without this the development of production and that enormous plan of capital undertakings which are contemplated for 1930–31 can not be assured.

This program of industrial development is inseparably connected with enormous new tasks for transport (rail and water), and puts before the latter such high demands as can not be fulfilled without the swiftest basic improvement of the whole organization of transport, and without the active participation in this matter of the whole mass of railroad and water transport workers and technical specialists.

In 1930–31 we must also guarantee Bolshevik rates of development of the socialist state and collective farm section of agriculture, the fulfilment of huge production programs by such organizations as the Grain Trust, the Cattle Trust, the Pig Trust and others, making provision for the developing socialist construction in the villages by a complete realization of the tasks in producing agricultural machines, tractors and chemical fertilizers.

The fulfilment of all this gigantic economic program is possible only if there is an immediate active mobilization of all the forces of the working class, all Party organizations, all trade unions, the whole Communist Youth and all economic organizations without exception. Not to understand this is to neglect a basic Bolshevik obligation in the cause of assuring the success of socialist construction, and represents a direct crime against the Party, especially on the part of the leaders of the above mentioned organizations.

The recognition in words of the general line of the Party and the failure in fact to take the most decisive and timely measures to mobilize the whole working class for the fulfilment of this economic program is unworthy of Bolsheviki, and represents the worst form of right opportunism in practice.

Only the immediate development of work for the preparation of the carrying out of the production program of industry next year can assure the development of the Bolshevik rates of development of industry, which were accepted by the 16th Party Congress.

The most important condition of the realization of the industrial financial plan for next year is the fulfilment of that plan for 1929–30. Bolshevik preparation for the fulfilment of the gigantic production program of the third year of the Five-Year Plan is rooted in the unconditional execution of the industrial financial plan of the present year.

The second year of the Five-Year Plan was a year of big achievements by socialist industry. Big socialist industry for ten months increased its production by 27% and displayed a pace of growth which set a record for the reconstruction period. Heavy industry — that basis of socialism —during the same period increased its production by 39.5%. The scope of capital construction for ten months is defined at 2,400,000,000 or 2,500,000,000 rubles.

But along with these successes and achievements we must not overlook the serious breach which was revealed in the course of the execution of the plan which was established by industry.

The growth of industrial production by 27% indicates a sharp declination from the increase of 32% which was prescribed by the plan. The plan was left unfulfilled not only in light industry, where this was caused to a certain extent during the present year by the lack of raw material, but also to a considerable extent in heavy industry, a fact which is especially important. The visible slackening of the work of industry during the last months created a direct threat of failure to carry out the annual production program, which was accepted by the Party and the Soviet power. Instead of Bolshevik rates of development, one observes in many branches of industry recently a disgraceful reduction of tempo and an opportunist tendency to drift with the tide.

The course of capital construction is also clearly unsatisfactory. Less than half of the plan of capital construction was fulfilled during the first three quarters.

Especially disgraceful is the lagging behind of capital building in the Building Union, the chemical and coke and gas industries, in the New Steel, the Machine Union and the agricultural machinery industry. These impermissible developments in capital building threaten the pace of development which has been undertaken and the fulfilment of the Five-Year Plan in four years.

The most important cause of the nonfulfilment of the productive tasks of industry, especially in its basic branches, is the absence of the necessary energy and initiative in the cause of mobilizing internal resources: insufficient use of existing equipment, low number of additional shifts, absence of energy in overcoming the shortages within an undertaking, frequent stoppage of equipment as a result of the failure to organize and adjust material and technical supply, the numerous accidents from criminal neglect and poor technical control, the absence of systematic work for rationalization and the extremely unsatisfactory character of planning within the factories. Instead of Bolshevik struggle with conservatism in the technical production management of the undertakings, instead of revolutionary vigilance against saboteurs and mobilization of the activity of the most advanced workers for cooperation in the development of the work of the undertakings, the economic managers often follow the advice of the more conservative of the specialists, and sometimes of out-and-out saboteurs. The managers do not properly support the more advanced of the engineers and technicians and hold aloof from the active workers, i. e., in practice limit themselves to bureaucratic methods of work.

The results of all this are reflected in the most negative fashion in general and agricultural machine building, in ferrous metallurgy and in the coal industry. Similarly, the possibility, which has been revealed, of doubling the machine building programs next year indicates how great are the unused reserves of capacity in our undertakings. The successful fulfilment of increased tasks by such enterprises as, for example, the Electrical Factory, the Southern Mining Industry (Krivoi Rog) and the old paper factories are a result of the struggle for the use of the internal resources of the plants.

However, there are still too few such examples, while examples of conservatism and bureaucratism in the use of the internal resources of industry are encountered at every step.

Numerous cases of clearly exaggerated requirements for imported equipment, without attempts to utilize the internal resources of industry, are one of the clearest illustrations of a bureaucratic attitude of the economic leaders toward their obligations, and to some extent reflect an opportunist lack of faith in the possibilities of socialist industry. Moveover, there are frequent and clearly unsubstantiated attempts to justify the nonfulfilment of industrial tasks by insufficiency of imported equipment. If our Party, trade union and economic organizations, following the example of certain plants, such as the Leningrad metal factory named after Stalin (in extending the construction of turbines), had shown real initiative in the matter of utilizing the productive resources of our factories, industry would have obtained supplementary opportunities not only for fulfilling, but for considerably exceeding, the plan.

In a number of cases, as in the oil industry, the mining industry of Ukraina and nonferrous metallurgy, the nonfulfilment of the production plan is caused first of all by the clearly unsatisfactory course of preparatory works — prospecting, drilling and sinking of shafts —, and this threatens the further development of these branches of industry. Such a situation is especially intolerable in view of the exceptional importance of these branches of industry.

Changes in the economic situation, reflected especially strongly in the question of labor power and its large turnover, had special significance for the fulfilment of the industrial plan in this year. The huge scope of socialist industrialization, the drawing into production in this connection of all the old trained workers and of an immense layer of new workers, especially from the village, and the simultaneous development of collective and state farm upbuilding, together with the increased harvest, brought the greatest changes in comparison with that period when there was still a considerable number of unemployed in the cities, and when the superfluity of free working hands was felt with especial sharpness in the little individual peasant households.

These changes in the situation, which were not taken into account by the economic organizations and the trade unions, on the one hand, brought into industrial enterprises a flow of new workers, who have not passed through the school of big production and who are not infrequently filled with petty bourgeois slacker sentiments, and, on the other hand, a withdrawal of a certain part of these workers into the villages in the time of field work and distribution of the harvest. Instead of taking actual account of the existing situation and adopting necessary measures (along the line of developing proletarian public consciousness, corresponding adaptation of the organization of workers' supply, rewarding the best producers, etc.) to attach the workers to the enterprises, and struggling decisively with the slacker elements who appeared casually in plants (people who ran from one place of employment to another, etc.), the economic organizations and trade unions and also the Party organizations displayed quite intolerable passivity in this matter and thereby permitted a considerable development of turnover in the labor force.

It is especially necessary to point out the bureaucratic attitude toward economic problems on the part of the departments of the Commissariat for Labor and also of certain trade unions. It is sufficient to say that when there was a visible shortage of workers in factories, mines and construction works in all industrial regions, the departments of the Commissariat for Labor, up till very recently, limited themselves to the printing of bureaucratic " data " about hundreds of thousands of unemployed, and paid out tens of millions of rubles in " unemployment " subsidies, without combatting slackers, loafers who declined work, etc.

The consumers' cooperatives revealed no less bureaucratism and incapacity for solving new problems. They were unable to reorganize their work in a fashion necessary to cope with the problem of attaching the workers to production, to mobilize their productive possibilities for really improving the supply of workers, to develop mass control of the working men and women over the work of all the departments of the cooperatives. Responsibility for this lies to a certain degree also on the departments of the Commissariat for Trade.

The clearest illustration of the confusion of the economic departments and trade unions and of their failure to take timely measures to combat the labor turnover, which was undermining labor discipline and bringing confusion into production, must be considered the situation which has arisen in connection with new economic circumstances with relation to labor power in the enterprises of the All-Union Coal Industry and the Urals, in a number of construction enterprises and even in some plants in Moscow and Leningrad. This situation has led to the biggest breaches in production programs.

The main and decisive deficiency in industrial work remains an inability to organize and lead the spontaneously growing activity of the working class. Notwithstanding the vast scope of socialist competition and the shock brigade movement in the factories, our economic, trade union, Young Communist and Party organizations often lag behind in this matter, and sometimes opportunistically follow after the active proletarians (e. g., Sormovo and others).

The development of socialist competition and the shock brigade movement is to a considerable extent promoted by bringing the tasks of the production program to the department, to the brigade, to the individual machine. At the same time, socialist competition and the shock brigade movement pass to a higher stage, on the basis of the development of proletarian activity, of the utilization of the productive achievements of the shock brigade movements and their rationalizing initiative, and also of a real practical reckoning with workers' proposals for the utilization of reserves of production power. This finds expression in the creation by the factory workers of the extra industrial financial plan, the significance of which lies in greater economy in the resources of the undertaking in carrying out the productive program, in raising the quality of production and especially in a further acceleration of a Bolshevik pace of industrial construction. The extra industrial financial plan acquires special significance as a method of really drawing all the workers into the cause of socialist construction, and as a most important means of struggle with counter revolutionary sabotage.

However, in point of fact in many cases the Party and other factory organizations not only do not give proper support to the workers' initiative in creating the extra industrial financial plan, but also fail suitably to organize socialist competition in its various and ever new forms (conveyor shock brigades, public supervision of one enterprise by another, etc). Without this it is impossible to guarantee a Bolshevik tempo for developing socialist industry. There are still many cases of false " shock brigade work " in industry and transport. There is still no small measure of formally bureaucratic attitude toward competition. There are still not a few members of the Party who do not understand the rôle and obligations of Communists in the plants as pacemakers in the struggle for the fulfilment of the industrial financial plan.

On the part of the economic directors who are in the really leading posts of socialist construction, there is often a lack of consciousness of their exceptional responsibility for their cause and a lack of understanding of their unconditional obligation to combine a firm realization of one-man management in the plant with the ability to rely in all their work on the Party, trade union and Young Communist organizations, on all the active Communist and nonparty workers.

The biggest failures of socialist competition and the shock brigade movement were reflected in the breaches of production plans which have been revealed, and in the very seriously threatened breach of the industrial financial plan of this year.

The situation which has arisen in industry demands decisive and immediate measures to mobilize the forces of the whole Party and the whole working class for the fulfilment of the industrial plan of the present year, which has been accepted by the Party. This is all the more necessary and incapable of postponement because the liquidation of the breach which has been uncovered in the industrial financial plan is the basic condition for guaranteeing the fulfilment of the production program of the third year of the Five-Year Plan.

Hence are derived the following fundamental problems of the Party and the whole working class:

(1) All forces of the Party, Young Communist and economic organizations and of the trade unions to concentrate on the development of the cause of socialist competition and the shock brigade movement, and on the support of the initiative of the workers in this cause in all its forms (conveyor shock brigades, public supervision, etc.); all forces to concentrate on the development of the extra industrial financial plan in factories, mines and construction enterprises, on railroad and water transport.

The Central Committee whole-heartedly supports the initiative of the All-Union Trade Union Council in organizing during September a developed campaign of the trade unions for the extra industrial financial plan, and in organizing on October 1 an All-Union " Day of the Shock Brigade Worker." The Central Committee points out that only if all trade union organizations are immediately and actually drawn into this campaign can it become a genuine means of liquidating breaches in the industrial plan, and assure the fulfilment of the production program.

(2) Immediately to carry out measures which guarantee a decisive strengthening of labor discipline and real struggle with disorganization and absenteeism. These measures must assure the swiftest actual change in the matter of raising the productivity of labor and the factual realization of one-man management in economic administration. Without this it is impossible to overcome the existing difficulties in industry.

(3) To guarantee the development of the initiative of the engineers and technicians in production and technical questions, and by every means to push forward the creation of

new trained experts from the working class, more boldly and consistently promoting leading workers, especially organizers of competitions, to responsible posts, overcoming in this connection conservatism, bureaucratism and opportunist lack of faith in the capacities of the working class.

(4) In order to combat labor turnover in the plants, to carry out a system of measures guaranteeing the attachment of the workers to the factories by means of a corresponding development of proletarian public opinion, the introduction of pledges of the workers themselves before this public opinion to work at a given enterprise for a minimum period and the application of all measures of social persuasion, including the boycotting of malicious deserters from production, and also the establishment of a system of various forms of rewards and supply, encouraging long periods of work at the factory.

In view of the lack of harmony between a number of laws, especially of the regulations about labor exchanges, and the present economic situation, immediately reexamine these laws with the idea of abolishing those which obstruct the struggle with labor deserters. Along with this assure the intensified drawing into production of the working class youth, and also of the wives of workers and other wage-earners.

(5) The organization of the workers' supply service has great significance in connection with the execution of the industrial financial plan.

For the purpose of improving distribution by the co-operatives, it is necessary to extend those practices which have justified themselves in application and which guarantee to the greatest degree the interests of the productive workers (reserved shops, attachment of worker members of coopera-tives to stores, merciless struggle with theft in the cooperative apparatus, more severe punishments for abuses in the use of food cards, etc.), and to push forward in industrial regions the organization of suburban dairy, vegetable and cattle farms. Party, trade union, Young Communist and economic organizations must show all kinds of aid to the development of the initiative of the workers in this matter, must improve the cooperatives, and by every means develop mass control of the workers over the functioning of the cooperatives.

(6) The press carried out on the basis of developing self-criticism much work in the cause of mobilizing the working masses for the fulfilment of the industrial financial plan. Along with this the press in many cases, by limiting itself to superficial campaign agitation, did not achieve a sharpening of the struggle against the decisive concrete deficiencies of economic work, and did not cope with the problem of timely organization of the masses to face the new problems raised by changes in the economic situation.

(7) Decisive struggle against slackening the pace of work in connection with summer vacations. In a number of economic organizations this assumed the disgraceful form of leaving institutions without guidance, and represented one of the serious obstacles to the fulfilment of the present industrial financial plan and the preparation for the third year of the Five-Year Plan. Without immediate and decisive elimination of this sort of demobilizationist sentiment, which represents one of the clear manifestations of opportunism in practice, the mobilization of the Party forces and the workers for the liquidation of the breach and the fulfilment of productive tasks will remain only a matter of words.

Such are the most important problems of the present day.

The production program of the present year and the economic projects of the third year of the Five-Year Plan mean a practical program of socialist construction and a development of the offensive against the capitalist elements along the whole front.

Notwithstanding the major deficiencies in the realization of productive tasks which have been revealed, socialist construction moves victoriously ahead, mercilessly smashing in its course all attempts at resistance by the class enemy (*kulaks*, counter revolutionary saboteurs, bourgeois restorationists, including such types as Groman, Kondratiev and Sukhanov). Panic-stricken right-wingers — those advocates of the *kulaks* —, Trotzkyist elements, who in fact are transformed from yesterday's " left-wingers " into actual accompanists of the right opportunists, and also persons who assume a conciliatory attitude toward the right-wingers and the Trotzkyists represent a bourgeois influence on the proletariat. Therefore, the infiltration into the Party of any kind of opportunist sentiments, undermining the fighting capacity of the proletariat in its developing offensive against the capitalist elements, must meet a decisive Bolshevik repulse. This is the basic condition of the victorious progress of socialism and, guaranteeing Bolshevik rates of socialist construction, is therefore a prerequisite for the overcoming of the difficulties which stand in the way of this construction.

The surmounting of the difficulties which confront us depends above all upon our work, upon our ability to carry on logical and uncompromising struggle with looseness, disorganization and bureaucratism in our organizations, and especially upon our capacity to mobilize the working class, which is a source of quickly growing and inexhaustible revolutionary energy, for the cause of the struggle for communism.

The industrial financial plan is threatened. This strikes at the program of the third year of the Five-Year Plan. We draw from this the Bolshevik conclusion:

All forces of the Party, all forces of the working class for the fulfilment of the industrial financial plan, for the guaranteeing of the program of the third year of the Five-Year Plan!

CENTRAL COMMITTEE OF THE ALL-UNION COMMUNIST PARTY (BOLSHEVIKI).

APPENDIX IV

Decree of the Central Executive Committee and Council of People's Commissars of the Union of Soviet Socialist Republics, dated December 15, 1930 [1]

PROCEDURE FOR THE ENGAGEMENT AND DISTRIBUTION OF LABOR AND THE CAMPAIGN AGAINST THE FLUIDITY OF LABOR

[Published in *Izvestia* of December 17, 1930]

The immense successes in the socialistic industrialization of the country and the rapid tempo of collective and state farm construction have brought about the complete liquidation of unemployment.

In this connection it has become necessary, simultaneously with the training of new labor cadres, to utilize more fully and rationally the existing labor forces in all branches of the national economy.

Planned utilization can only give the best results if it is coupled with measures permitting the wider extension of socialistic forms and methods of work (socialist competition, shock brigade tactics, etc.). At the same time planned utilization of labor is impossible without a decisive and

[1] *A Selection of Documents relative to the Labour Legislation in force in the Union of Soviet Socialist Republics*, p. 176 (London, His Majesty's Stationery Office, Russia No. 1 (1931) Cmd. 3775).

195

systematic campaign against all disorganizing elements in production.

In view of the above, the Central Executive Committee and the Council of People's Commissars of the Union of Soviet Socialist Republics decree:

1. Labor organizations are charged with the duty of insuring the planned distribution of labor within the limits approved by the competent planning organs.

2. All undertakings, institutions, organizations and individuals are obliged to engage workers and employees only through the labor organizations, except in the cases mentioned in this decree.

3. The employment of persons who have passed through higher educational institutions or technical schools is effected in accordance with the special laws regarding their allocation to employment.

4. The People's Commissariat of Labor of the Union of Soviet Socialist Republics shall fix the category of persons to be registered with labor organizations as seeking employment, and the procedure to be followed in placing them in employment. In this connection it should be borne in mind that persons who by their social position are nearest to the working classes should be set to work in industry and transport.

5. As an exception to Art. 2 of this decree, the following persons may be engaged without resort to the labor organizations:

(a) Responsible administrative-technical workers and specialists;

(b) Workers leaving one undertaking, institution or economic organization for another with the consent of the management of the undertaking, institution or organization in which they are employed;

(c) Apprentices to handicraft workers, or to craftsmen working on their own or employing not more than two hired workers;

(d) Poor peasants, male or female, in one-man peasant farms, and shepherds in peasant farms;

(e) Domestic servants;

(f) Other workers, by special agreement with the labor organizations.

Lists of the situations for which, in accordance with (a), the employer is permitted to engage workers directly, and also the procedure for making agreements under (f) shall be fixed by the People's Commissariat of Labor of the Union of Soviet Socialist Republics.

6. Labor agreements for a definite period may be concluded for a period not exceeding three years.

7. Skilled workers and specialists found in undertakings of the socialized sector not to be employed in the work for which they are specially qualified shall be redistributed by labor organizations in accordance with the procedure laid down by the People's Commissariat of Labor of the Union of Soviet Socialist Republics, in conjunction with the Supreme Council of National Economy of the Union of Soviet Socialist Republics, the People's Commissariat of Ways and Communications and the All-Union Council of Trades Unions.

8. In order to insure a supply of skilled workers and specialists for enterprises of the most important branches of the national economy (iron and steel, coal and chemical industries, machinery construction, capital construction, transport, and the electrical industry) at the expense of the less

important branches or the less important undertakings of such branches, the People's Commissariat of Labor of the Union of Soviet Socialist Republics has the right, on notifying the economic organizations and in agreement with the trade unions, to carry out, with the sanction of the Council of Labor and Defense, the transfer of skilled workers and specialists to other branches of the national economy or to other localities for utilization in the work for which they are specially qualified.

9. Managers of undertakings are obliged to release, at times fixed by the labor organizations, workers who are obliged to leave for work in other undertakings in the circumstances mentioned in Arts. 7 and 8.

10. The Council of People's Commissars of the Union of Soviet Socialist Republics is charged with the giving of guarantees for workers transferred to other undertakings in the cases mentioned in Arts. 7 and 8, as regards the reservation of their living quarters in their former, and the provision of living quarters in their new place of residence, provision for the acceptance of their children in schools, children's homes and playgrounds, and the payment of their traveling expenses, in addition to other pecuniary inducements.

11. Workers and engineer-technical workmen who have distinguished themselves as organizers of " shock brigades," members of brigades or participants in socialist competition, as well as those who have worked in one undertaking for a considerable time or those who have made valuable suggestions regarding rationalization or who have produced inventions, enjoy the following privileges:

(a) If they are living in unsatisfactory quarters, they have priority in obtaining living accommodation in the living quarters reserved for the undertaking;

(*b*) Their children have priority for vacancies in the higher educational institutions, technical schools, courses, etc.;

(*c*) They have priority for vacancies in homes of rest, sanatoria, etc.;

(*d*) They have priority of dispatch to other undertakings in the Union of Soviet Socialist Republics or abroad for studying manufacture and raising their qualifications;

(*e*) Members of their families, when applying for work to the labor organizations, are given employment by these organs preferably in those undertakings where the workers themselves are employed.

12. All workers directly engaged in production work in the mining, metal, chemical and textile branches of industry, in industries producing building materials, on rail, water and motor transport, and in important constructional work, if they have worked in the same undertaking or constructional work uninterruptedly for not less than two years after November 1, 1930, receive annually an additional three days' leave of absence or compensation to the extent of three days' wages.

The transfer of a worker to another undertaking in accordance with the instructions of the administration or labor organization does not affect the above-mentioned two years' period.

13. Malicious disorganizers of output, who leave their work in the socialized sector without authorization and without satisfactory excuse, are not, in the event of their applying for work to labor organizations, given employment in industry or transport for a period of six months.

The People's Commissariat of Labor of the Union of Soviet Socialist Republics is instructed to define within one month the category of persons falling within the purview of this article.

14. Persons registered with the labor organizations who refuse without satisfactory excuse to accept employment on work for which they are specially qualified, and to which they are directed by the labor organizations, are removed from the register for a period of six months.

15. Managers of undertakings, institutions and economic organizations in the socialized sector are liable, in accordance with the fixed regulations, to disciplinary penalties on the instructions of higher organizations or to administrative penalties on the order of labor organizations for the following offenses:

(a) For the improper utilization of skilled labor in undertakings, institutions or economic organizations;

(b) For applying for or utilizing labor above the requirements fixed by the financial plan of industry;

(c) For failing to take due steps to insure the supply of labor for undertakings, institutions and organizations;

(d) For infringing the standards of wages fixed in collective agreements or by the state;

(e) For inducing workers and administrative-technical personnel to leave one undertaking for another undertaking or organization;

(f) For detaining workers or administrative-technical personnel whose transfer has been ordered by the labor organizations.

16. The Council of People's Commissars of the Union of Soviet Socialist Republics is charged to issue within 20 days a list of the laws of the Union of Soviet Socialist Republics that are canceled by the issue of the present decree, and amendments of the laws of the Union of Soviet Socialist Republics arising therefrom.

The Government of the allied republics are requested

within one month to introduce in their legislation the changes arising from the present decree.

17. The Council of People's Commissars of the Union of Soviet Socialist Republics is charged to carry out within 20 days, and in accordance with this decree, the reorganization of the organs in charge of the labor returns.

President of the Executive Committee of the Soviet Union
M. KALININ

President of the Council of People's Commissars of the Soviet Union
A. I. RYKOV

Secretary of the Central Executive Committee of the Soviet Union
A. YENUKIDZE

Moscow, December 15, 1930.   52/691.

APPENDIX V

Decree of the People's Commissariat of Labor of the Union of Soviet Socialist Republics, October 9, 1930.   No. 314 [1]

REGARDING THE IMMEDIATE DISPATCH OF ALL UNEMPLOYED TO WORK AND THE CESSATION OF PAYMENT OF UNEMPLOYMENT BENEFIT

[Published in *Izvestia*, November 11, 1930.   No. 281]

The People's Commissariat of Labor decrees as follows:

1. In view of the great shortage of labor in all branches of state industry, insurance bureaus are requested to discon-

[1] *A Selection of Documents relative to the Labour Legislation in force in the Union of Soviet Socialist Republics*, p. 165 (London, His Majesty's Stationery Office, Russia No. 1 (1931) Cmd. 3775).

tinue payment of unemployment benefit. No provision for the payment of unemployment benefit has been made in the Budget of Social Insurance for the supplementary quarter October-December, 1930.

2. Labor exchanges are instructed to take all necessary measures in order that the unemployed be immediately sent to work, and of these the first to be sent are persons entitled to draw unemployment benefit.

3. Unemployed persons are to be drafted not only to work in their own trades, but also to other work necessitating special qualifications.

At the same time labor exchanges, according to local conditions (the needs of any particular trade) should extend their activities in the training and retraining of unemployed.

4. No excuse for refusal of work, with the exception of illness, supported by a medical certificate, should be considered. Refusal of work carries with it removal from the registers of the labor exchanges.

Medical certificates should be issued to the unemployed by medical boards and medical control boards. Unemployed in possession of medical certificates will receive benefits under the heading of unemployment benefit, but this benefit will come out of the sums allocated for temporary incapacity.

5. The personal responsibility for the due and correct execution of the present decree is placed upon the heads of the labor exchanges (and in districts where these are not in existence on the directors of labor organizations) and upon the chairmen of insurance bureaus.

6. Art. 1 of the present decree is to be put into force by telegraph.

APPENDIX VI

Resolution of the Central Committee of the All-Union Communist Party [1]

CONCERNING THE TEMPO OF COLLECTIVIZATION AND MEASURES OF STATE AID IN THE BUILDING OF COLLECTIVE FARMS

1. During the last months the collectivization movement made a new stride forward, taking in not only separate groups of individual households but also whole regions, districts and even territories. At the basis of the movement lies the collectivization of the means of production of the poor and middle class peasant households.

All the rates of the development of the collectivization movement indicated by the plans have been exceeded. By the spring of 1930 the planted area cultivated on a socialized basis will considerably exceed 30,000,000 hectares. So the Five-Year Plan of collectivization, according to which it was proposed to include 22,000,000 or 24,000,000 hectares in collective farms by the end of the Five-Year Plan, will be considerably more than fulfilled, even in the present year.

So we possess the material basis for the replacement of big *kulak* production by big production of the collective farms and a powerful advance toward the creation of socialist agriculture, to say nothing of the state farms, the growth of which runs considerably ahead of all the planned proposals.

This circumstance, which has decisive significance for the whole economic life of the Soviet Union, gave the Party full reason in its practical work to pass over from the policy of limiting the exploiting tendencies of the *kulaks* to the policy of liquidation of the *kulaks* as a class.

[1] Translated from *Rabochaya Gazeta*, January 7, 1930.

2. On the basis of all this it may be affirmed with confidence that, within the bounds of the Five-Year Plan, instead of collectivizing the 20% of the sown area contemplated under the Five-Year Plan we can decide the problem of collectivizing the enormous majority of the peasant households. The collectivization of the most important grain regions, such as the Lower Volga, the Middle Volga and the North Caucasus, may be basically completed by the autumn of 1930 or, in any event, by the spring of 1931; the collectivization of the other grain regions may be basically finished by the autumn of 1931 or, in any case, by the spring of 1932.

3. In conformity with the growing tempo of collectivization it is necessary still more to intensify the work of building factories which produce tractors, combines and tractor accessories, so that the dates set by the Supreme Economic Council for finishing the construction of new factories should in no case be postponed. Moreover, the Central Committee proposes to the Supreme Economic Council to inform the Central Committee, not later than March 15 of this year, about measures which will guarantee by next year both the further growth of the general measures of production of complicated agricultural machines in old factories, and also especially a considerable increase of the output of tractor and complicated horse-drawn equipment.

4. Inasmuch as the decision concerning the problem of the replacement of horse-drawn equipment by equipment of a mechanical type can not be fulfilled in a short time and requires a number of years, the Communist Party Central Committee demands that there should be a decisive rejection of the tendency to estimate inadequately the rôle of horse-drawn machinery, a tendency which leads to the dispersion and selling off of horses. The Central Committee emphasizes the extraordinary importance, under present conditions and

as a transition measure, of creating in the collective farms horse-machinery bases and a mixed type of tractor-horse bases, combining tractor with horse-drawn equipment.

5. In connection with the growing tempo of the collectivization movement, the Central Committee proposes to the Soviet Commissariat for Agriculture a regrouping of the land settlement forces and resources in such a manner as to guarantee fully the land settlement needs of regions of complete collectivization, postponing individual land settlement, with the exception of some minor nationality regions and some regions of the consuming belt, where the collectivization movement has not yet developed broadly.

6. In accordance with the foregoing considerations, the Central Committee considers it absolutely necessary to increase the general sum of credit for the collective farm section from 270,000,000 rubles to 500,000,000 rubles, correspondingly reducing the credits of other sections.

7. In accordance with the change of conditions in regions of complete collectivization, the machine-tractor stations, united by the All-Union Tractor Center, must reorganize their work on the basis of: (a) contracts pre-eminently, if not exclusively, with collective farms; and (b) the obligation of the peasants to cover the value of the stations in the course of three years.

At the same time, in regions where the state farms are widely separated (for instance, the Middle Volga and certain districts of the North Caucasus), there must be experiments with a type of combined farm, with the state farm as its fundamental basis, operating both under contract conditions and for pay, and helping the collective farms which conclude contracts with it, especially in tractor sowing and machine harvesting.

8. In view of the special importance of trained leaders,

the Central Committee proposes to the Soviet Commissariat for Agriculture, to the Collective Farm Center and to the regional committees of the Party that they hasten the work of developing trained leaders for the collective farms, and supply the latter with these leaders, creating for this purpose a broad network of accelerated courses. Attract to these accelerated courses first of all people with practical experience in the collective farm movement from the peasants and members of the workers' brigades who have proved themselves organizers of the collective farm movement.

9. The experience of complete collectivization in the given stage of collective farm development demonstrates that the most widespread form of collective farm is not the cooperative for the common working of the land — in which private property rights in the means of production are preserved, while labor is socialized — but the agricultural *artel*, in which are collectivized the *basic* means of production (working animals and machinery, agricultural buildings, marketably productive cattle). Consequently, the Central Committee commissions the Soviet Commissariat for Agriculture to work out, with the broad cooperation of the collective farm organizations, in the shortest possible time a model constitution for the agricultural collective farm *artel*, as a form transitional to the commune, taking account in this connection of the impermissibility of admitting *kulaks* into collective farms.

10. The Party organizations must head and organize the collective farm movement, which is spontaneously growing from below, with the purpose of assuring the organization of *really collectivist production* in the collective farms, so as not only to obtain the extension of the planted area and growth of the harvest yield indicated by the plan but also to make the present sowing campaign a point of departure

for a new upswing in the collective farm movement, in accordance with the decision of the November plenary session of the Central Committee.

11. The Central Committee emphasizes the necessity of decisively combatting any attempts to hold back the development of the collectivization movement for lack of tractors and complicated machines. At the same time the Central Committee very seriously warns Party organizations against any " decreeing " of the collective farm movement from above; this might create a danger of replacing genuine socialist competition in the organization of collective farms by mere playing at collectivization.

APPENDIX VII

Decision of the Central Executive Committee and Council of People's Commissars of the Soviet Union, February 1, 1930

MEASURES FOR STRENGTHENING THE SOCIALIST REORGANI-
ZATION OF AGRICULTURE IN REGIONS OF COMPLETE
COLLECTIVIZATION AND FOR STRUGGLE WITH THE *Kulaks*

For the purpose of guaranteeing the most favorable conditions for the socialist reconstruction of agriculture the Central Executive Committee and Council of People's Commissars of the Soviet Union decide:

1. In regions of complete collectivization to stop the operation of the law as regards the leasing of land and the employment of hired labor in individual peasant holdings. (Seventh and eighth divisions of the general rules about land exploitation and land arrangement.)

Exceptions from this rule in regard to middle class households are regulated by regional executive committees under the guidance and control of higher district executive committees.

2. To grant to territorial executive committees and to governments of autonomous republics the right to apply in these regions all the necessary measures of struggle with the *kulaks* up to the complete confiscation of the property of the *kulaks* and the expulsion of the latter from the confines of the respective regions and territories.

The confiscated property of the *kulaks*, with the exception of that portion which goes for the settlement of debts owed by the *kulaks* to state and cooperative organizations, must be transferred to the reserve funds of the collective farms to cover the entrance fees of the poor peasants and farm laborers who are entering the collective farms.

3. To propose to the governments of the republics of the Soviet Union, in developing the present decision, to give the necessary instructions to the territorial executive committees and to the governments of the autonomous republics.

President of the Central Executive Committee
of the Soviet Union
M. KALININ

President of the Council of People's Commissars
of the Soviet Union
A. I. RYKOV

Secretary of the Central Executive Committee
of the Soviet Union
A. YENUKIDZE

KREMLIN, MOSCOW, February 1, 1930.

APPENDIX VIII

Final Text accepted by the Central Collective Farm Administration. Approved by the Commissariat for Agriculture, and confirmed by the Council of the People's Commissars of the Union of Soviet Socialist Republics and the Presidium of the Central Executive Committee of the Union of Soviet Socialist Republics

MODEL ARTICLES OF ASSOCIATION FOR AGRICULTURAL *Artels* [1]

[Collection of Laws of the Union of Soviet Socialist Republics, 1930. No. 24, Chap. 255. Published in *Izvestia* (No. 60) of the TS. I. K. of the Union of Soviet Socialist Republics and of the Vtsik of March 2, 1930]

I. PURPOSES AND OBJECTS

1. We, poor peasants (*bednaki*) and middle peasants (*serednaki*) of the village of .... in the district of .... in the area of ...., of our own free will, unite in an agricultural *artel* so that our united means of production and our common organized labor may be used for the purpose of forming a large collective economic entity, and in this manner insure a complete and effective victory over the *kulak*, over all exploiters and enemies of the workers, over poverty and ignorance, over the backwardness of individual economic entities, and create a high labor output and marketable surplus by collective means.

II. LAND

2. All boundaries separating the arable holdings of the members of the *artel* are to be removed, and all pasture

---

[1] *A Selection of Documents relative to the Labour Legislation in force in the Union of Soviet Socialist Republics*, p. 115 (London, His Majesty's Stationery Office, Russia No. 1 (1931) Cmd. 3775).

holdings are to be run together into one single area for the collective use of the *artel*.

When pooling all the holdings, homesteads (orchards, gardens, etc.) are to be left for the individual use of the members of the *artel*, and where necessary the size of such homestead is to be adjusted by a decision of the management of the *artel* and confirmed by a general meeting.

3. The area of land of the *artel* is in no case to be diminished. No land can be withdrawn from the pool by a member leaving the *artel*. Those leaving the *artel* can only obtain land from the free lands of the state.

III. MEANS OF PRODUCTION

4. The following are communized: All draft animals, agricultural implements, all other livestock, all seed reserves, fodder in such quantities as is necessary for the feeding of the common livestock, farm buildings necessary for the running of the *artel* farm, and all agricultural plant. Living quarters of the members of the *artel* are not communized.

When communizing agricultural implements, such small agricultural implements as are required for working the homestead are left for the individual use of the member of the *artel*.

From the communized draft animals, the management of the *artel*, if necessary, will allot a minimum number of horses for the individual use of the members of the *artel*.

When there is only one cow in the holding, it is not communized. In the case of a holding having a number of cows, one cow is left for the individual use of the member of the *artel*, and the remainder are communized. Productive livestock is in all cases communized. An *artel* dairy is formed with the communized milking cattle.

In areas where small livestock farming (i.e., pig and sheep) is carried on, the small livestock is communized, but a certain number of animals are left for the individual use of the member of the *artel*, in numbers to be decided by the *artel*. In areas where there is no small livestock farming, pigs and sheep are not communized. Poultry is not communized.

Apart from the small livestock and poultry left to individual ownership, collective farms organize small stock and poultry enterprises.

To insure the *artel* against a bad harvest, or shortage of fodder, emergency seed and fodder reserves are formed.

IV. ACTIVITIES OF THE *Artel*

5. The management and members of the *artel* undertake the following obligations:

(*a*) To increase the amount of land under cultivation by making use of all the land available, by improving and cultivating waste land, and by rationally organizing the exploitation of their holding.

(*b*) To make full use of all motive power, all implements, all tractors, all machines, seeds and other means of production; purchase with their own means, and means borrowed, tractors and other means of production in order in course of time completely to mechanize the farm.

(*c*) To arrange for the proper use and upkeep of all livestock and implements; and to see that the collective livestock and implements are kept in better condition on collective farms than those in private ownership.

(*d*) To improve pasture and arable land and take the agricultural measures necessary for the increase of the yield.

(*e*) To take the necessary technical and veterinary

measures to increase and improve the selling value of the livestock and poultry.

(*f*) To develop all other branches of agricultural production with due regard to the natural conditions of the locality, and to develop handicrafts in accordance with local conditions.

(*g*) To organize building construction and the collective basis of farm and public buildings and auxiliary institutions.

(*h*) To raise the cultural and political level of members of the *artel*.

(*i*) To improve the living conditions of the members of the *artel*, especially of the women and children.

V. MEMBERSHIP

6. Admission to membership of the *artel* is decided by the management, which submits a list of the new members for approval at the next general meeting. Appearance in person by workers permanently employed outside the *artel* is not compulsory.

7. Any worker, upon reaching the age of 16, can become a member of the *artel*.

Kulaks and persons who have been deprived of their electoral rights are not eligible for membership of an *artel*. Exceptions to this rule are permitted for members of families among whose members are to be found persons loyal to the Soviet régime, red partisans, soldiers of the Red Army, sailors of the Red Fleet (of all ranks) or village male or female teachers on condition that they stand surety for their families.

Peasant families who, before entering a collective group, slaughter or sell their livestock, get rid of their implements or with ill intent dispose of their seed, are not admitted.

VI. RESOURCES OF THE *Artel*

8. Each person entering the *artel* must deposit an entrance fee of from 2% to 10% of the value of all property, whether communized or not, falling to his share of the holding, with the exception of articles of domestic or personal use.

In cases where the principal source of income of the person entering the *artel* is from wages (agronomists, teachers, surveyors, employees in institutions or organizations situated in the neighborhood of the *artel*), the amount of the entrance fee is fixed in each case by the management, but must not exceed 10% of his annual income.

The entrance fee for agricultural laborers shall not exceed five rubles. Workers who are permanently employed outside the collective farms shall pay an entrance fee of 3% of their annual wages in addition to the entrance fee of from 2% to 10% of the value of their property provided for in the articles of association.

Note. From a working member of the *artel*, no additional deduction from wages is made over and above the entrance fee to the *artel*.

Payment of the entrance fee by instalments may be permitted by the management only in accordance with rules and for periods laid down by the collective farm union. The entrance fees are credited to the reserve fund of the *artel*.

9. From the value of the communized property of a member of the *artel* (draft and productive livestock, implements, farm buildings, etc.), from 25% to 50% is credited to the reserve fund of the *artel* in such a way that the wealthier peasant households pay a higher rate of contribution to the reserve fund. The balance of the value of the property is reckoned as the share of the member of the *artel*.

10. The management settles accounts with a member who leaves the *artel* and returns his share to him, but the person

leaving the *artel* is only entitled to receive land outside the area of the collective farm. Accounts are made up as a rule at the end of the economic year.

11. Out of the income of the *artel* at the end of the economic year provision is made for the expenses of running the *artel*, for the support of persons who are unfit for work, for the reserve and other communal funds (from 10% to 30% to the reserve fund, and from 5% to 15% for other communal funds) and for the payment of labor.

VII. ORGANIZATION AND PAYMENT OF LABOR

12. All the work in the *artel* is carried out by the personal labor of its members, in accordance with the internal regulations approved by a general meeting. Only persons having specialized knowledge or training (agronomists, engineers, technicians, etc.), may be brought in for hired employment on agricultural work.

The hire of temporary labor is allowed only in exceptional cases when urgent work can not be performed within the required time by the members of the *artel* working to their full capacity, and also in case of building work.

13. Each member is allotted his work by the management of the *artel* in accordance with the internal regulations. No member may refuse to do the work allotted to him.

14. For the proper organization of the work of the members of the *artel*, standards of output and costing schedules shall be laid down, records shall be kept of the quality and quantity of work, and payment by piece and task work shall be adopted.

15. Payment for the labor of the members of the *artel* shall be made according to the following rules:

In the course of the economic year advances (in kind or

money) shall be made to the members of the *artel* for food and other necessities, but not more than 50% of the amount due to them for their work. At the end of the economic year a final settlement as regards remuneration for labor is made.

Note. Out of the sums earned by members of the *artel*, who are working outside the *artel*, deductions are made for the communal funds of the *artel* to the amount of from 3% to not more than 10%; the deduction within these limits is fixed either by the *artel* or collective farm group.

16. The *artel* gives assistance to those members who are unable to work and to those who are temporarily incapacitated. The conditions and amount of such assistance is decided by the management of the *artel* and approved by a general meeting, in accordance with the economic resources of the *artel*, but not in excess of the average wage.

VIII. Sanctions

17. All members of the *artel* undertake to conform to the stipulations of the articles of association, to the decisions of the management and of the general meeting, to observe the internal regulations, and scrupulously to perform tasks allotted to them by the management and their communal duties.

Unbusinesslike or negligent treatment of communal implements and livestock is regarded by the *artel* as treachery to the cause of collectivization and as practical support of the enemy, the *kulak*.

For such unbusinesslike or negligent treatment of communal property, for failing to report for work without adequate reason, and for other breaches of discipline, the management imposes penalties upon the offenders in accordance with the internal regulations (*e. g.*, reprimand, warning, temporary suspension from work, fine, etc.). If a member is found incorrigible, the management shall submit to the general meeting the question of his expulsion from membership of the *artel*.

IX. MANAGEMENT OF THE AFFAIRS OF THE *Artel*

18. The affairs of the *artel* are conducted by the general meeting of members and by the management. If the calling of a general meeting is difficult owing to the large number of members or widely scattered dwellings, a general meeting is replaced by a meeting of delegates. Members of the meeting of delegates are elected at a general meeting of members of the *artel*, by the several groups of dwellings of the collective farm.

19. The general meeting (or meeting of delegates) is the supreme organ for the conduct of the *artel*. It decides the most important questions as regards the functioning of the *artel*, elects the management and the supervisory commission, and confirms the instructions in connection with their work.

The general meeting (or the meeting of delegates) can only conduct business when there are not less than half the total number of members present. Decisions of a general meeting (or meeting of delegates) are taken by a majority and by a showing of hands.

20. The management of the *artel* is elected for one year, is the executive organ of the *artel* and manages all its affairs. The management allots among its members duties in regard to the direction of the business and production of the *artel*, places upon the various members of the management complete responsibility for the duties allotted to them, and invests them with the necessary powers.

The management must keep accounts according to the forms and rules laid down for the collective system.

21. The supervisory commission supervises the work of the management, in particular the observance of the articles of association, the execution of the production plan and of agreements with and obligations to the state, audits cash, property, documents and records, reports upon the annual statements, and renders an account of its work to the general meeting (or meeting of delegates).

X. Mutual Relations of Units within the System

22. The *artel* shall become a member of the ....
.... Collective Group and shall carry on its work under its direct guidance.

On the basis of its production plan the *artel* shall conclude with the .... Collective Group an agreement (concerning the obligations of the *artel* as regards the organization of agricultural production), the delivery of all produce to the state and to cooperatives, and also the obligations of the collective group and of other state and cooperative organs as regards the supply to the *artel* of means of production and articles of utility, and as regards the organization of credit assistance and of agricultural technical services for the *artel*.

APPENDIX IX

Concerning the Struggle with Distortions of the Party Policy in the Collective Farm Movement [1]

To all Central Committees of National Republics, to All Territorial, District and Regional Committees of the Party:

[1] Translated from *Izvestia*, March 15, 1930.

Information about the collective farm movement received in the Central Committee of the Party shows, along with real and very substantial successes of collectivization, that there are observed instances of the distortion of the Party policy in various regions of the Soviet Union.

Above all, the principle of *voluntariness* in building up the collective farms is violated. In a number of regions voluntariness is replaced by compulsion to enter the collective farms under the threat of expropriation, deprivation of electoral rights, etc. As a result, into the number of those expropriated as *kulaks* part of the middle class and even of the poor peasants sometimes fall. In some regions the percentage of expropriation rises to 15, and the percentage of persons deprived of electoral right to 15 or 20. Cases are observed of exceptionally rough, disorderly and criminal treatment of the population by some of the minor officials, who are sometimes victims of provocation on the part of masked counter revolutionary elements (banditism, division of property, arrest of middle class and even poor peasants, etc.). In a number of regions preparatory work for collectivization and patient explanation of the bases of Party policy to the poor and middle class peasants are replaced by bureaucratic official decreeing from above of swollen figures, and by an artificial inflation of the percentage of collectivization. (In some regions collectivization in a few days " rises " from 10 to 90%.)

Such practices are a violation of the well-known instruction of Lenin to the effect that collective farms can be vital and firm only if they grow up on a voluntary basis. The decision of the 16th Congress of our Party concerning the impermissibility of applying compulsory measures in organizing collective farms is violated. There is a violation of the constitution of the agricultural *artel*, confirmed by the Council of People's Commissars and the Central Executive Committee of the Soviet Union, in which it is expressly stated that the farm laborers, poor and middle class peasants of such and such a village " *voluntarily* unite in an agricultural *artel*."

Along with these distortions are observed in some places inadmissible and harmful instances of *compulsory* socialization of houses, small animals, chickens and milk cattle without market value, and in connection with this attempts at stupid jumping over from the *artel* form of collective farms, which is the basic link of the collective farm movement, to the commune. It is forgotten that our basic agricultural problem is not the " chicken " or the " cucumber " problem, but the *grain* problem. It is forgotten that the basic link of the collective farm movement at the present moment is not the commune, but the *agricultural artel*. It is forgotten that just for this reason the Party found it necessary to issue a model constitution not for an agricultural commune, but for an agricultural *artel*. As a result of these stupid distortions we have in a number of regions a discrediting of the collective farm movement and a withdrawal of the peasants from a number of hastily patched up and therefore completely unstable *artels* and communes.

Consequently, the decision of the Party that the basic link in the collective farm movement at the present moment is not the commune, but the *artel*, is violated. There is a violation of the well-known decision of the Central Committee of the Party of January 6, 1930 (see *Pravda*) that the *artel* form of the collective farm movement is its main form, and that consequently one must not permit a frivolous jumping from the *artel* form to the commune.

Finally, the Central Committee considers it necessary to note the quite inadmissible distortions of the Party line in the field of struggle with religious prejudices, and also in the sphere of goods exchange between city and village. We have in mind here cases of the *administrative* closing of churches without the agreement of the overwhelming majority of the village, which usually leads to a strengthening of religious prejudices, and the abolition in a number of market places and bazaars, which leads to a deterioration in the supply of the cities. There can be no doubt that such a practice, carried out under the flag of the " left " phrase, in reality pours water on the mill of counter revolutionists and has nothing in common with the policy of our Party.

The Central Committee considers that all these distortions are the result of a *direct violation* of the policy of the Party, of a *direct violation* of the decision of the guiding organs of our Party, which can only create soil for strengthening the " right " elements of the Party.

The Central Committee considers that all these distortions are now the *basic obstruction* to the further growth of the collective farm movement and a *direct help* to our class enemies.

The Central Committee considers that further *quick growth* of the collective farm movement and *liquidation of the kulaks* as a class are *impossible* without immediate *liquidation* of these distortions.

The Central Committee makes it obligatory for Party organizations:

1. To stop the practice, observed in a number of places, of forced methods of collectivization, and simultaneously carry on further persistent work for *attracting* the peasantry into the collective farms on a voluntary basis and *strengthening* the existing collective farms.

2. To concentrate the attention of Party workers on the economic improvement of the collective farms and the organization of field work, guaranteeing by corresponding

220

economic and Party political measures the reinforcing of the successes which have been achieved in collectivization and the economic organization of the agricultural *artel*.

3. Not to permit the transfer of agricultural *artels* to the constitution of agricultural communes without the confirmation of district collective farm unions or district executive committees, and to stop the *forced* socialization of dwellings, small cattle, birds and unmarketable milk cattle.

4. To examine the lists of persons who have been expropriated and deprived of electoral rights and to correct without delay the mistakes which were committed in this field in regard to middle class peasants, former Red partisans and members of families of village teachers and officers and soldiers and sailors of the Red Army and Navy.

5. While adhering strictly to the rule of not admitting *kulaks* and other persons deprived of electoral rights into the collective farms, to *permit exceptions* from this rule for members of those families which include Red partisans, officers, soldiers and sailors of the Red Army and Navy, and village teachers, who are devoted to the Soviet power, provided that these vouch for the members of their family.

6. To *forbid* the closing of markets, to *reestablish* bazaars and *to refrain from checking* the sale by peasants, including members of collective farms, of their products on the market.

7. Decisively to *stop* the practice of closing churches administratively, with a fictitious justification of a voluntary desire on the part of the population. To *permit* the closing of churches only in the event of the real desire of the overwhelming majority of the peasants, and only with the confirmation of the decisions of the peasant meetings by territorial executive committees. To hold guilty persons to

strictest responsibility for mocking the religious feelings of peasant men and women.

8. To remove from their posts and replace with others those Party workers who are not able or do not desire to carry out a decisive struggle with distortions of the Party policy.

CENTRAL COMMITTEE OF THE
ALL-UNION COMMUNIST PARTY

APPENDIX X

Decision of the Central Committee of the All-Union Communist Party of April 2, 1930 [1]

CONCERNING ADVANTAGES FOR COLLECTIVE FARMS

1. To propose to the Council of People's Commissars and the Central Executive Committee of the Soviet Union:

(a) To free from tax liability for two years all the socialized working animals in the collective farms (horses, oxen, etc.);

(b) To free from tax liability for two years cows, pigs, chickens and sheep, both those collectively owned by the collective farm and those in the individual possession of its members;

(c) To establish for socialized gardens and garden collective farms a 50% reduction from the rates of garden income established for the given region. Land which is newly planted in socialized gardens and garden collective farms are to be free from the agricultural tax for two years;

(d) According to these decisions, correspondingly to reduce the general sum of the agricultural tax for 1930–31.

[1] Translated from *Izvestia* of April 3, 1930.

2. To propose to the Council of People's Commissars of the Soviet Union to guarantee the complete fulfilment of the decision of the Party Central Committee of January 5 about crediting the collective farms in the present year to the extent of 500,000,000 rubles.

For the purpose of improving the material position of the collective farms:

(a) To postpone until the end of the business year the covering of the delayed indebtedness on credits which fall on farms entering the collective farm, and also of the delayed indebtedness assumed by the collective farms on behalf of the peasants who entered them. This indebtedness may be repaid in instalments in accordance with the receipt of incomes from crops and cattle;

(b) To cancel for collective farm members indebtedness in connection with the land arrangement which was in effect before they entered the collective farm;

(c) To cancel all fines and court sentences connected with the nonfulfilment of agricultural obligations, nonpayments, etc., imposed upon peasants entering the collective farms before April 1, 1930;

(d) To carry out the collection of share capital and deposits in credit societies and cooperatives only on a voluntary basis, forbidding the practice, which occurred in a number of cases, of compulsory contributions;

(e) To forbid the practice of collecting by compulsion deposits in savings banks, which has been observed in some regions;

(f) To consider as finished the collection of subscriptions for tractors in the current business year;

(g) To free the collective farms from the payment of debts on the confiscated *kulak* property which has passed into the possession of the collective farms.

3. To propose to the Commissariat for Trade to forbid the taking for slaughter, according to contracts, of cows with calf from one-cow households which belong to collective farms.

4. To propose to the Collective Farm Center:

(a) To forbid the deduction for the benefit of the collective farms from the incomes of members outside the collective farm of a greater percentage than is established by law in regard to incomes from supplementary trades (from 3 to 10% of the earnings), irrespective of the time and place of work;

(b) To make it obligatory for the managing boards of collective farms not to place obstructions in the way of collective farm members who desire to work during time which is free from collective farm work with the socialized collective farm horses on hauling, lumbering and other jobs. Forty per cent of the earnings of the collective farm member remains in his possession if he uses fodder which belongs to the collective farm, while he keeps 60 or 70% if he feeds the horse with his own fodder.

5. To propose to the Council of People's Commissars of the Soviet Union to annul all decisions of the central organs not in conformity with this decision.

APPENDIX XI

Resolution on the Collective Farm Movement and the Development of Agriculture, unanimously adopted by the 16th Congress of the All-Union Communist Party on July 13, 1930

[*Excerpt*]

CONCERNING THE TEMPO OF COLLECTIVIZATION AND THE PROBLEMS OF REORGANIZING AGRICULTURE [1]

The course of development of the spring sowing of 1930 shows that, on the basis of collectivization and the establishment of collective farms, the Party will succeed in solving the very difficult grain problem. The solution of the grain problem in its turn not only facilitates the development of nongrain crops and cattle breeding, but also solves the question of the possibility, by means of the development of collective and state farming, of bringing the backward branches of agriculture out of the difficulties which are insuperable for small farms with low productivity.

The possible rates of the further development of grain cultivation and of the surmounting of the crisis in cattle breeding are defined by those enormous possibilities of the development of productive forces which the collective farms contain in themselves.

Last spring not only the machine tractor station and the old collective farms, but also the new collective farms, based upon the simple throwing together of peasant machinery and as yet lacking adequate experience in organization and farming, were able considerably to extend their sown area and to plant waste land. Moreover, the possibilities opened

[1] Translated from *Krasnaya Zvyezda* of July 15, 1930.

up by the development of the state farms are indicated by the fact that the old and new state farms alone will even this year yield about 100,000,000 poods (about 1,667,000 tons) of marketable grain, and next year will yield not less than 250,000,000 poods. This shows that, on the basis of collectivization, development of machine tractor stations and organization of state farms, the Party can begin to achieve the slogan of "overtaking and outstripping" the capitalist countries of the world not only in regard to industry, where the advantages of large scale management have long been revealed with enormous force, but also in the field of agriculture, where the tempo of development hitherto has been determined by the overwhelming predominance of very slightly productive small farms and now will be determined by the accelerated development of collective and state farms, representing a new type of farming unknown in the history of humanity and first discovered by the experience of economic construction in the Soviet Union.

In accordance with this the Congress considers it necessary :

1. Fundamentally to reconsider the Five-Year Plan of agricultural development, taking as a basis the tempo of collectivization contemplated by the decision of the Central Committee on January 5, which has been fully confirmed by experience, in order on this basis to guarantee, along with the hastened development of grain and other crops, the increase and intensified development of cattle-breeding, above all by the organization of special state cattle-breeding farms, analogous to the state grain farms, as well as by the widespread creation of collective farms with a high marketable surplus and by the quick extension of the fodder supply.

2. Along with the steady observance of the advantages for collective farms and their members contemplated by the decisions of the Party, to increase the credits for collective

farms in 1930–31 so as to double the figure for the present year, i. e., to make it a billion rubles.

3. To guarantee the sowing by the Grain Trust next year of not less than 4,500,000 hectares and the preparation for sowing of 9,000,000 hectares in 1932.

4. To guarantee a market supply by the Pig Trust of not less than 400,000 pigs in 1930–31, not less than 3,000,000 in 1931–32 and not less than 7,000,000 in 1932–33.

5. To bring up the number of head of cattle of the " Skotovod " (a state cattle-raising organization) to 3,200,000 in 1930–31, 5,500,000 in 1931–32 and 9,000,000 or 10,000,000 in 1932–33.

6. To develop cattle-raising branches in the collective farms, assigning a considerable part of the agricultural credits for this purpose.

7. In view of the fact that a combination of the tractor with the horse on field work will be required for a number of years, it is necessary to take good care of horses and to create suitable regions for special state farms and cooperatives devoted to horse-breeding.

8. To commission the Lenin Agricultural Academy to work out the following questions: Rational distribution of agriculture in the territory of the Soviet Union according to branches and crops; replacement of less advantageous by more advantageous crops; guaranteeing the Soviet Union, along with the possibility of an independent supply in the main food and raw material crops, the possibility of maximum exploitation of local power sources in agriculture.

In connection with the problems referred to the Lenin Agricultural Academy, to create for its work the necessary technical basis, on the level of the latest achievements of science, and to insure its strengthening with Communist leaders.

9. To develop the work of the Collective Farm Institute, so that its work may guarantee a timely scientific and practical elaboration of forms and methods of collective farm development and a theoretical generalization of local experience.

10. To assure the complete fulfilment of the program of tractor and combine construction, the production of spare parts and tractor accessories in amounts defined by the decisions of the Central Committee; and also increased production of mineral fertilizers, especially of means to combat insect pests.

To turn special attention in this connection upon the improvement of the quality of tractor machinery.

APPENDIX XII

Resolutions Adopted by the United Plenary Session of the Central Committee and Control Commission of the All-Union Communist Party, December 17–21, 1930 [1]

ECONOMIC PROBLEMS

1. Regarding Economic Life as a Whole:

(a) To fix tentatively the national income of the Soviet Union for 1931 as 49,000,000,000 rubles (in prices of the year 1926–27) as against the figure of 49,700,000,000 rubles, which was proposed for the last year of the Five-Year Plan (1933), so that the growth of the national income in 1931 would constitute not less than 35% (as against a growth of national income by 19% in 1930 and by 11% in 1929).

[1] Translated from *Izvestia* of December 22, 1930.

(b) Assuming this growth of national income, to define the capital investments in the socialized section of national economic life (industry, agriculture, transport, etc.) at 17,000,000,000 rubles, instead of 10,000,000,000 rubles as in the past year.

(c) To fix the value of industrial goods of wide consumption for 1931 at 14,600,000,000 rubles, as against 11,500,000,000 rubles in 1930 (a growth for the year of 3,100,000,000 rubles, as against a growth in 1929–30 of 1,000,000,000 over the preceding year). This, along with the growth of the supply of agricultural products, must increase the retail turnover by 25 or 30% over the preceding year.

2. Regarding Industry and Electrification:

(a) To establish the scope of capital construction in socialist industry and electrification (regional electric stations) for 1931 at 7,470,000,000 rubles, of which 850,000,000 rubles are to be assigned to electrification and 5,500,000,000 rubles to the industry which is planned by the Supreme Economic Council. (Of the latter sum, 500,000,000 rubles are to be assigned to the reserve of the Supreme Economic Council for industry and electrification.)

To fix the reduction of building costs at 12%.

(b) To set the growth of the total output of all state industry (under the Supreme Economic Council and the People's Commissariat for Supply) at 45% by comparison with 1930. This means the fulfilment of the whole Five-Year Plan of industrial production by 79% in the third year of the Five-Year Plan, 1931. For the branches of heavy industry the plan will be fulfilled by 98%.

(c) To bring the general power of all operating electrical stations up to 4,500,000 kilowatts by the end of 1931 and to bring the production of electrical energy up to 12,700,000,000 kilowatt-hours, as against 8,800,000,000 kilowatt-hours in 1930.

(d) To establish for the industry which is planned by the Supreme Economic Council a growth in the number of workers by 10%, in the productivity of labor by 28% and a reduction of production costs by 10%, with obligatory improvement of the quality of production. The corresponding figures for the industries planned by the Commissariat for Supply are: increase in the number of workers by 16% and of productivity of labor by 35%, with reduction of production costs by 11%.

3. Regarding Agriculture:

(a) To guarantee in 1931 the inclusion in collective farms of not less than 80% of the peasant households in the steppe region of Ukraina, in the North Caucasus, the Lower Volga and the Middle Volga (Trans-Volga). This means for these regions the completion, on the whole, of full collectivization and liquidation of the *kulaks* as a class. To guarantee for the other grain regions — the Central Blackearth Region, Siberia, the Urals, Ukraina (the wooded-steppe districts) and the grain regions of Kazakstan — 50% collectivization of the peasant households. For the consuming belt 20 or 25% of the grain farms are to be collectivized. To assure the collectivization of not less than 25% of the peasant households in the cotton and sugar beet regions.

To guarantee, on the average for the Soviet Union in all branches of agriculture in 1931, the collectivization of not less than half of the peasant households.

(b) To bring up the general amount of land sown with all crops in 1931 to 143,000,000 hectares (spring [1] and winter sowings of 1931).

---

[1] *Cf. Economic Review of the Soviet Union*, VI, p. 99.

To fix the sown area of the state farms at 9,500,000 hectares (5,000,000 hectares for the state farms of the Grain Trust) and of the collective farms at not less than 66,000,000 hectares, of which not less than 50,000,000 hectares are to be under spring crops.

(c) To increase the number of machine-tractor stations of the Tractor Center by the end of the year to 1,400 with a general figure of 980,000 horsepower.

(d) To create 2,800,000 head for the Cattle Trust, 1,900,000 head for the Pig Trust, and 4,400,000 head for the Sheep Trust; to supply the Milk and Butter Trust with 110,000 cows.

(e) To fix the scope of investment in the socialized section of agriculture (state and collective farms) at 3,800,000,000 rubles, 2,055,000,000 rubles for the state section and 1,745,-000,000 rubles for the collective farms and machine tractor stations.

4. Regarding Transport and Communication:

(a) To accept as the figure of freight to be transported on the railroads in 1931 the figure of 330,000,000 tons, as against 281,000,000 tons proposed for the last year of the Five-Year Plan.

(b) To assure a reduction in the costs of shipments of not less than 9% during 1931.

(c) To take 3,185,000,000 rubles as the sum of capital investments in transport.

(d) To take 135,000,000 rubles as the sum of investments in civil aviation (besides 15,000,000 rubles which are assigned for exploitation purposes).

(e) To assign 260,000,000 rubles for investment in communications during 1931.

5. Regarding the Commissariat for Supply and Consumers' Cooperation:

To define the amount of capital investments at:

(a) 230,000,000 rubles for the Commissariat for Supply (raw material base, elevators, cold-storage plants, warehouses, etc.).

(b) 365,000,000 rubles for the Consumers' Cooperatives (public feeding, suburban gardens, store construction, etc., without industry).

6. Regarding Labor and Education:

(a) To establish the general number of workers and employees in 1931 at 16,000,000, as against 14,000,000 in 1930.

(b) To set the growth of wages in 1931 by comparison with 1930 at 6% for industrial workers and 8% for transportation workers. To fix the year's fund for wages in 1931 at 15,300,000,000 rubles, as against 12,500,000,000 rubles in 1930.

(c) To fix the year's fund of social insurance for workers and employees in 1931 at 2,138,000,000 rubles (as against 1,600,000,000 rubles in 1930). This exceeds the program for the last year of the Five-Year Plan (1,950,000,000 rubles).

(d) To establish the size of the fund for improving the living conditions of the workers in 1931 at 285,000,000 rubles, as against 125,000,000 rubles in 1930.

(e) To assign 155,000,000 rubles for the protection of labor in industry and transport.

(f) By the end of 1931 to put on the seven-hour working day all railroad workers, not less than 92% of the workers employed in that industry planned by the Supreme Economic Council, and 52% of the workers in that industry planned by the Commissariat for Supply.

(*g*) To place on the five-day working week during 1931 all workers in the industries which are planned by the Supreme Economic Council, with the exception of the textile workers, and 98% of the workers in the industries which are planned by the Commissariat for Supply.

(*h*) To invest in housing construction in all branches of socialized economic life 1,100,000,000 rubles, as against 582,500,000 rubles last year.

(*i*) To appropriate 6,500,000,000 rubles, as against 5,000,000,000 rubles in 1930, for financing education, science, health, social welfare and the training of experts.

7. Regarding the Financial Plan:

1. To estimate the sum of the unified financial plan (budget, credit system and independent resources of the economic organizations) at 31,100,000,000 rubles of income and 29,600,000,000 rubles of expense (in this figure the state budget is to reckon with 21,200,000,000 rubles of income and 19,700,000,000 rubles of expense). Income is to predominate over expense and a state reserve to the amount of 1,500,-000,000 rubles is to be created.

2. Appraising the facts that

(*a*) the successes of a planned socialist economic system have made it possible in the sphere of finance to adopt the system of a unified financial plan, embracing all the resources of the country devoted to capital building, filling out the turnover mechanism of the socialized economic system, education, administration and defense of the Soviet Union;

(*b*) the unified financial plan embraces and redistributes about two thirds of the whole national income for the cause of socialist construction;

(*c*) the successful fulfilment of the financial plan and the

budget are directly dependent upon the fulfilment of the quantitative and qualitative indices in all branches of economic construction;

(*d*) without strict fulfilment of the financial plan the achievement of the indicated economic plan in all branches of economic life is impossible:

The plenary session considers indispensable the decisive strengthening of the work of all financial organs, the introduction of the strictest financial discipline and economy, the unconditional realization of items of income, the establishment of the direct dependence of the expenditures of every organization upon the fulfilment of its production and financial plans, the strengthening of the ruble and energetic struggle against the tendency to underestimate the rôle and significance of the financial system in the present stage of socialist construction.

APPENDIX XIII

Decree adopted at the Third Session of the Fifth Central Executive Committee of the U. S. S. R.

THE UNIFIED FINANCIAL PLAN AND UNIFIED STATE BUDGET OF THE U. S. S. R. FOR 1931 [1]

Having heard and considered the report of the Council of People's Commissars of the Soviet Union and of the Budget Commission of the Central Executive Committee of the Soviet Union on the Unified Financial Plan and the Unified State Budget of the Soviet Union for 1931, the Third Session of the Central Executive Committee of the Soviet Union decides:

[1] Translated from *Izvestia* of January 12, 1931.

Section I

1. To approve the following statement of revenues and expenditures of the Unified Financial Plan of the Soviet Union for 1931:

BALANCE SHEET OF THE UNIFIED FINANCIAL PLAN, 1931

Revenues

Rubles

I. Revenue from the socialized sector of the national economy:

1. Industry	4,076,000,000	
2. Electric power plants	140,000,000	
3. Agriculture	1,094,000,000	
4. Timber	70,000,000	
5. Municipal enterprises	773,000,000	
6. State trade	1,480,000,000	
7. Consumers' cooperatives	779,000,000	
8. Transportation	3,381,000,000	
9. Communications	136,000,000	
10. Credit institutions	932,000,000	
11. Economic organs of the Commissariat for Finance	61,000,000	
12. Special funds of departments and institutions supported by state and local budgets	106,000,000	
13. Miscellaneous	365,000,000	
		13,393,000,000

II. Revenue from Taxation:

1. General state	10,843,000,000	
2. Local	435,000,000	
		11,278,000,000

III. Revenue from insurance organizations:

1. Social Insurance	2,174,000,000	
2. State Insurance	490,000,000	
		2,664,000,000

Rubles

IV. Revenue from individual citizens:
1. Loans... 1,300,000,000
2. Voluntary contributions................ 400,000,000
3. Cooperative deposits and dues 921,000,000
4. Savings banks 400,000,000
5. Bonds of Tractor Center.............. 160,000,000
6. Repayment of loans advanced by
   the All-Union Cooperative
   Credit Bank............................... 700,000,000
   ———————— 3,881,000,000
V. Revenue from trade unions........ 400,000,000
VI. Miscellaneous revenue................ 302,000,000

Total Revenues.................. 31,918,000,000

Expenditures

I. Financing national economy:
1. Industry.. 7,991,000,000
2. Electrification.............................. 865,000,000
3. Agriculture 4,833,000,000
4. Municipal and housing construc-
   tion... 815,000,000
5. Housing cooperation...................... 100,000,000
6. State trade.................................... 2,183,000,000
7. Consumers' cooperatives.............. 525,000,000
8. Transportation.............................. 3,310,000,000
9. Civil aviation................................ 150,000,000
10. Communications........................... 260,000,000
11. Economic organs of the Commis-
    sariat for Finance..................... 30,000,000
12. Miscellaneous............................... 37,000,000
    ———————— 21,099,000,000
II. Financing social and cultural enterprises:
1. Education....................................... 3,516,000,000
2. Health.. 1,189,000,000

		Rubles	
3.	Labor protection and social welfare	1,012,000,000	
4.	Administrative expenses	68,000,000	
			5,785,000,000
III.	Commissariat for War and Navy		1,310,000,000
IV.	Administration		696,000,000
V.	Reserve funds		430,000,000
VI.	Loan payments		382,000,000
VII.	State insurance		286,000,000
VIII.	Miscellaneous expenditures		430,000,000
	Total Expenditures		30,418,000,000
	State Reserve Fund		1,500,000,000
	Grand Total		31,918,000,000

SECTION II

2. In accordance with the above balance sheet of the Unified Financial Plan for 1931, to confirm the draft of the Unified State Budget of the U. S. S. R. for 1931 as submitted by the Council of People's Commissars of the Soviet Union, introducing into it the following changes, proposed by the Budget Commission of the Central Executive Committee of the U. S. S. R.:

[Here follows a list of minor alterations in the budget appropriations.]

3. The 1,500,000,000 rubles excess of income over expenditures to be devoted to the creation of a reserve fund for the Unified State Budget of the Soviet Union.

4. As a result of all the changes adopted to confirm:

(a) The subjoined statement of revenues and expenditures of the Unified State Budget of the U. S. S. R. for 1931:

UNIFIED STATE BUDGET, 1931 [1]

I. *Revenue*

Rubles

A. Revenue from taxation:
1. Single agricultural tax................... 500,000,000
2. Business turnover tax.................... 9,393,000,000
3. Trade and industry tax................ 180,000,000
4. General income tax....................... 300,000,000
5. Excess profits tax......................... 18,000,000
6. Customs duties and other customs revenues............................ 302,000,000
7. Special tax for cultural needs 150,000,000
  Total..................................   10,843,000,000

B. Revenue not derived from taxation:
1. Industry....................................... 1,559,400,000
 (156,800,000 rubles derived from local industry)
2. Electrical power plants................. 48,200,000
3. State farms.................................. 57,700,000
4. Enterprises under the People's Commissariat for Internal Supply... 349,200,000
5. Enterprises under the People's Commissariat for Foreign Trade.. 700,000
6. Other trading enterprises............. 12,913,000
7. Enterprises under the Commissariat for Transportation.......... 59,900,000
8. Enterprises under the Commissariat for Finance...................... 34,000,000
9. Banks........... 181,000,000
10. Consumers' cooperatives.............. 537,000,000
11. Producers' cooperatives................ 44,000,000
12. Special cooperatives for the disabled.. 1,700,000

[1] This budget is compared with that for 1930 in *Economic Review of the Soviet Union*, **VI**, p. 147.

		Rubles	
13.	Agricultural cooperatives	708,000	
14.	Housing cooperatives	591,000	
15.	State property	46,145,000	
16.	State insurance	23,200,000	
17.	Special commodity fund	600,000,000	
18.	Other revenue	97,261,000	
19.	Revenue from coin issue	20,000,000	
	Total		3,673,618,000
C.	State loans		1,700,000,000
	(including 400,000,000 rubles from savings bank resources)		
D.	Revenue from other sources:		
1.	Commissariat for Transportation	4,811,200,000	
2.	Commissariat for Posts and Telegraphs	480,000,000	
3.	Repayment of loans advanced for the financing of agriculture out of the budget of 1929–30	17,000,000	
4.	Revenue from local budgets	249,200,000	
	Total		5,557,400,000
	Total Revenues		21,774,018,000

II. Expenditures

A.	Financing National Economy:	
1.	Industries under the Supreme Economic Council	4,850,800,000
2.	Other industries	455,000,000
3.	Regional power plants	736,100,000
4.	Local power plants	32,325,000
5.	Agriculture	2,361,301,000
6.	Repayment of loans to finance agriculture out of the budget of 1929–30	17,000,000
7.	Enterprises under the Commissariat for Foreign Trade	196,900,000
8.	Enterprises under the Commissariat for Internal Supply	1,214,600,000

		Rubles	
9.	Commissariat for Transportation	4,569,500,000	
10.	Accumulated funds in the current account of the Commissariat for Transportation in the State Bank	54,200,000	
11.	Civil aviation	150,000,000	
12.	Road construction, from budgets of the constituent republics	34,200,000	
13.	Commissariat for Posts and Telegraphs	556,400,000	
14.	Municipal and housing construction	30,600,000	
15.	Other enterprises	38,955,000	
16.	Regulation of national economy	45,884,000	
	Total		15,343,765,000
B.	Social and cultural enterprises:		
1.	Education	1,104,031,000	
2.	Health	80,316,000	
3.	Labor protection and social welfare	45,422,000	
4.	Administration of social and educational work	9,224,000	
	Total		1,238,993,000
C.	Army and Navy		1,290,000,000
D.	Special militia		100,000,000
E.	Administration		231,143,000
F.	Reserve funds:		
1.	Reserve funds of the Councils of People's Commissars	379,800,000	
2.	Other funds	26,090,000	
	Total		405,890,000
G.	State loans		394,500,000

H. Transfer of funds to:

	Rubles	
1. Social insurance	35,000,000	
2. State insurance	20,000,000	
3. Local budgets	1,314,727,000	
Total		1,369,727,000
Total (A–H)		20,374,018,000
Reduction in administrative expenses		100,000,000
Total Expenditures		20,274,018,000
State Reserve Fund		1,500,000,000
Grand Total		21,774,018,000

(b) To confirm the statement of revenues and expenditures of the All-Union budget for 1931 at 18,687,686,000 rubles of revenue and 17,187,686,000 rubles of expenditures, assigning 1,500,000,000 rubles to the creation of a reserve fund.

(c) To confirm the statements of state revenues and expenditures to be assigned to the budgets of the constituent republics for 1931 in the following sums: 1,574,787,000 rubles for the Russian Soviet Federated Socialist Republic; 662,164,000 rubles for the Ukrainian Soviet Socialist Republic; 173,596,000 rubles for the White Russian Soviet Socialist Republic; 276,859,000 rubles for the Transcaucasian Soviet Socialist Republic; 96,351,000 rubles for the Turkoman Soviet Socialist Republic; 216,886,000 rubles for the Uzbek Soviet Socialist Republic; 85,689,000 rubles for the Tadjik Soviet Socialist Republic.

5. To assign to the budgets of the constituent republics deductions from the business turnover tax in the following amounts: Russian Soviet Federated Socialist Republic, 131,997,000 rubles; Ukrainian Soviet Socialist Republic, 98,812,000 rubles; White Russian Soviet Socialist Republic,

87,542,000 rubles; Transcaucasian Soviet Socialist Republic, 194,338,000 rubles; Turkoman Soviet Socialist Republic, 82,171,000 rubles; Uzbek Soviet Socialist Republic, 140,613,-000 rubles; Tadjik Soviet Socialist Republic, 74,063,000 rubles.

SECTION III

The transition to the system of a unified financial plan in the sphere of financial planning, first achieved in 1931, is a very great step forward in the strengthening and further completion of the whole system of planned socialist economic life of the Soviet Union.

The Unified Financial Plan of the Soviet Union in 1931 is inseparably connected with the whole economic plan of that year. Embracing on its revenue side almost 32,000,000,000 rubles and redistributing for socialist construction two-thirds of the whole national income, this plan sets vast organizing and operating problems before all the financial and economic organizations of the country.

If the successful fulfilment of the financial plan is directly dependent upon the fulfilment of the qualitative and quantitative tasks of the national economy of the country, all the production and building plans of 1931, in their turn, are guaranteed only in the event of the complete realization of the program of mobilization and redistribution of resources which is marked out in the financial plan.

Noting the increasing significance of the financial system at the present stage of socialist construction and approving the transition to the Unified Financial Plan, the Central Executive Committee proposes to the Council of People's Commissars of the Soviet Union and to the governments of the constituent republics:

1. To organize the work of economic and financial or-

ganizations in 1931 in such fashion as to give first place to the following tasks:

(a) The complete fulfilment of the quantitative and qualitative tasks of the economic plan of 1931;

(b) Maximum mobilization of the resources of the country, necessary to guarantee the pace of socialist construction which has been set;

(c) The carrying out of the strictest financial discipline and regime of economy in all branches of the national economy, social and cultural upbuilding and administration.

2. To make the payment of the expenses of all state institutions and economic organizations directly dependent upon their fulfilment of the financial and production plans which have been established for them.

3. To entrust the supervision and control of the fulfilment of the financial plans and estimates of the various departments to the Finance Commissariats of the Soviet Union and of the constituent republics and their local organs, making it obligatory for all departments and institutions, and also economic enterprises and organizations of the socialized sector, to submit to the financial organs in proper time all necessary data concerning their progress in carrying out the financial plans.

*President of the Central Executive Committee
of the Soviet Union*
M. KALININ

*Secretary of the Central Executive Committee
of the Soviet Union*
A. YENUKIDZE

MOSCOW, KREMLIN, January 10, 1931.

INDEX

INDEX

249

INDEX

INDEX

INDEX